Junks of Central China

Wu-Shan Shen-Po-Tzu

Junks of Central China

THE SPENCER COLLECTION OF MODELS
AT TEXAS A&M UNIVERSITY

Text by J. E. SPENCER

Photographs by JIM BONES, JR.

Foreword by EDWIN DORAN, JR.

TEXAS A&M UNIVERSITY PRESS

College Station and London

Copyright © 1976 by Texas A & M University Press

Library of Congress Cataloging in Publication Data

Spencer, Joseph Earle.
　　Junks of Central China.

　　　Bibliography: p.
　　　Includes index.
　　　1. Junks—Models—Exhibitions. 2. Yangtze
River—Navigation—Exhibitions. 3. Texas.
A & M University, College Station. 4. Spencer,
Joseph Earle. I. Texas. A & M University, College
Station. II. Title.
VM371.J85　　　623.82′01′2　　　75-40888
ISBN 0-89096-015-1 (cloth)
ISBN 1-58544-018-3 (pbk.)

Manufactured in the United States of America
FIRST PAPERBACK EDITION

Contents

Foreword 11

Preface 13

Junk Types of the Yangtze River Basin 17

  Regionalism in Junk Styles 20

    The Estuarine Transition Zone 20

    The Wuhu-Hankow Yangtze River Section 23

    Poyang Lake 23

    Tungting Lake–Hunan 23

    The Han River 24

The Middle River 26

The Yangtze Gorges–Upper River 26

Szechwan 29

Navigation of a Crooked-Stern Junk 31

Junk Construction 33

The Collection of Models 37

Plates 39

Selective Bibliographic Notes 99

Index 101

List of Plates

1. Kan-Ch'uan   41

2. P'ing-T'iao-Tzu   43

3. Wu-Chiang-Tzu   45

4. Ma-Yang Pa-Kan   47

5. Chung-Yen-Pan   49

6. Ch'an-Tzu   51

7. Lao-Ho-K'ou Ch'iu-Tzu   53

8. Hsiang-yang Pien-Tzu   55

9. Ching-Pang Hua-Tzu   57

10. Ching-Pang Hua-Tzu   59

11. Ching-Pang-Ch'uan   61

12. Pien-Ho Hua-Tzu   63

13. T'o-Pien-Tzu   65

14. Shui-Pao-Chia Fei-Hsieh   67

15. Fan-Kuan-Ch'uan   69

16. I-Chang Po-Ch'uan   71

17. I-Chang Hua-Tzu   73

18. I-Chang Lung-Ch'uan   75

19. Wu-Pan   77

20. Yu-Cheng-Ch'uan   79

21. Shou-K'ou Ma-Yang-Tzu   81

22. Shou-K'ou Ma-Yang-Tzu   83

23. I-Chang Ma-Yang-Tzu   85

24. Ma-Yang Kua-Tzu-Ch'uan   87

25. Pa-Tung Hsiao-Ho-Hua-Tzu   89

26. Hsiang-Chi Tou-K'ou   91

27. Wu-Shan Shen-Po-Tzu   93

28. Wai-P'i-Ku   95

29. Lao-Hua-Ch'iu   97

List of Illustrations

Wu-Shan Shen-Po-Tzu   *frontispiece*

Junk on Lower River with sail common to
    freshwater craft in the Yangtze Delta.   21

Fishing boat near Shasi showing sail
    characteristic of Central China waters.   21

Szechwan square sail.   22

Two *Lao-Hua-Ch'iu* on the Kialing River,
    with mat sails.   22

Yulohs and bow steering sweep being worked
    on a *Shou-K'ou Ma-Yang-Tzu* in the gorges.   23

Five oarsmen in working stance.   24

The river front at Hsiangyang.   25

A variant of the *Pa-Wan-Ch'uan* on the Kialing
    River with mat sail made of reed and
    bamboo.   27

A variant of the *Tao-Pa-Tzu* from the Lien
    River in central Hunan.   27

Lower section of the Ichang Gorge.   27

Junks at Ichang with rain mats protecting
    the decks.   27

A freshly oiled *Shou-K'ou Ma-Yang-Tzu*.   28

Stern of a *Shou-K'ou Ma-Yang-Tzu*.   28

A small *wupan* and trackers at a rapid.   30

Five junks working upstream on the lower
    Pa River.   34

An old Ichang lighter with bulkheads exposed.   35

Full-balance rudder of a *Shou-K'ou Ma-Yang-Tzu*.   35

An Ichang *T'o-Pien-Tzu* loading stone in the
    Ichang Gorge.   35

An Ichang *T'o-Pien-Tzu* propelled by two yulohs.   35

An Ichang *T'o-Pien-Tzu* with steering sweep
    in use.   36

MAP
Regional junk types of the Yangtze River Basin.   18

Foreword

SOME fifteen years ago I discovered that Joseph E. Spencer, Professor of Geography at the University of California at Los Angeles, owned a collection of Chinese junk models. As more facts were learned about the size, beauty, and uniqueness of the collection it occurred to me that maintaining the group of models intact in a permanent home and on public display would be an important contribution to nautical culture history. Over the years, at professional meetings and once when our paths crossed in Taiwan, I made something of a nuisance of myself with Joe Spencer by pursuing this goal. At last, recognizing the potential usefulness to a future wider audience, he agreed to let Texas A&M University have the collection. In September, 1974, in a ceremony appropriately graced by Dr. Spencer's presence and remarks, we placed on display the Spencer Collection of Model Chinese Junks.

Upon attainment of the first goal another imme-diately replaced it. Hundreds of persons have admired and studied the display of model junks in the past year but only a relatively limited number can hope to see the actual models. Why not publish an illustrated guide which would make the collection more widely accessible? This idea received approval and financial support from the Vice President for Academic Affairs, Dr. John C. Calhoun, Jr. The photographs of the models were made with great care and artistry by Mr. Jim Bones. The map was prepared by Michael F. Doran. Dr. Spencer courteously agreed to write the text, which explains the background of water transportation in inland China and describes each model in turn. Thus, from many sources and by many twists and turns, this volume has come into being. I believe it constitutes a major addition to our understanding of Chinese watercraft and trust that many others will find it both beautiful and useful.

EDWIN DORAN, JR.

Preface

PEOPLE sometimes become involved in particular undertakings without having ultimate objectives in mind. So it was with my wife, Kathryn, and me when we purchased our first models of Chinese junks in 1934. We then lived right on the river front at the edge of the busy Yangtze River port of Ichang; we both liked ships and boats and found the river traffic of absorbing interest; and the models were attractive decorative pieces in our living room. Letters to friends at home generated requests that we bring several of them junk models when next we returned to the United States. Conversation with a model builder about the nature of Chinese junks, in the interests of having the intended gifts executed as accurately as possible, put the business on something more than the original casual basis.

Personal photographs taken in the course of official travel duties on the Yangtze River were shown the model builder and produced some more models. A project concerned with the nature of the flow of trade in the Yangtze Basin involved inquiry into native transportation systems, in which I learned a great deal about the regional traffic patterns of the Central China junk trade. This knowledge proved helpful in discussions with the model builder about a particular type of junk, and it often resulted in another model being added to the collection. And so it went for almost two years, until we began to think about the problems of packing for an impending home leave. A steamer trunk and a suitcase apiece could serve the four people then involved, but the

junk models already on hand would need two huge wooden packing cases. At that point the collection abruptly stopped growing.

In the United States several basements and attics, over the years, provided effective storage space for the junk fleet, for which no significant purpose turned up. One particular attic was so satisfactory a storeroom that years went by with only an occasional change of one of the models in our living room. A slowly increasing knowledge of the collection brought offers from friends and others to buy one or more models, including a commercial offer for the whole fleet. All such offers were rejected, for by the late 1950's it had become evident that our collection was unique and should not be broken up. The house with the most satisfactory attic was finally sold in 1971, and at that point we decided we should find a permanent home for our collection of Chinese junk models. Edwin Doran, being under a spell as to nautical matters, also knew about the collection, of course, and for years had been at me about it. The uniqueness of our collection now afforded an ultimate objective to the original undertaking—that of placing the set of models where they could be properly displayed and utilized, to illustrate the variety of Chinese craft employed in trade on the different waters of the central Yangtze River system. We sincerely hope that an undertaking so casually commenced may finally prove to have lasting value and that this volume may be one phase of that display. Thanks are due to Edwin Doran for his persistence

Junks of Central China

Junk Types of the Yangtze River Basin

THE Yangtze River system, east of the high Tibetan border zone, includes on the order of one hundred tributary streams and canalized flood channels and many small to large lakes that are navigable by some kind of watercraft. Excluding the maze of canals constructed in the Yangtze Delta, the total mileage of navigable waterways approaches 20,000. Many of the larger tributaries have numerous navigable branches each, so that hundreds of big and little rivers form the usable drainage network of the Yangtze River system. The almost 1,800 navigable miles of the Yangtze River itself, below Pingshan on the edge of the Tibetan border, form the main artery of a water transportation system that long has carried more boat traffic than any other of the earth's great rivers. Within the navigable course of the Yangtze alone there are several sections of the river, each of which presents physical conditions and historic administrative controls different from those on any other section. Each of the lower courses of the tributaries has one or more sets of particular characteristics of channel conditions, seasonal variation in depth and flow patterns, and impediments to navigation. And, as one ascends those tributaries, not only do the conditions change but each of the "little rivers" near the headwaters of navigation displays its own unique set of conditions.

Pingshan, at the head of navigation on the Yangtze River itself, is at an elevation of something over 800 feet, so that the lower courses of the larger tributaries are chiefly at low elevations, and craft of considerable size and freight capacity can operate on them. Ichang, at the foot of the Yangtze Gorges and almost a thousand miles from the sea, is but 140 feet above sea level, and from here on down to the sea much of the floor of the Yangtze Basin constitutes a watery maze of flood channels and flood-reservoir lakes during the summer high-water season that has always made land transportation difficult. During the winter low-water period, many of the lakes shrink in size and become quite shallow, but most of them have flow channels that permit varieties of boat traffic. The main flood channels, long canalized to a fairly high degree, remain navigable during winter periods. There never is a problem of ice impeding traffic in winter within the Yangtze Basin.

Within the basin human ingenuity at an early date apparently was more effectively applied to devising locally suitable watercraft than to developing effective modes of land transportation. In consequence, until the modern era, when roads were built for wheeled vehicles, land transportation of commodities was relatively costly compared with water transportation. The particular problems of navigating the rivers and lakes were solved in some fashion a long time ago. The several local regions have very old traditions of building boats or rafts in specific ways both to meet local physical conditions and to handle specific commodities, such as coal, rice, fish, salt, cotton, and timber. Further, styles of watercraft were often devised to lessen the tax toll exacted under rules of measurement at control stations. It is my estimate

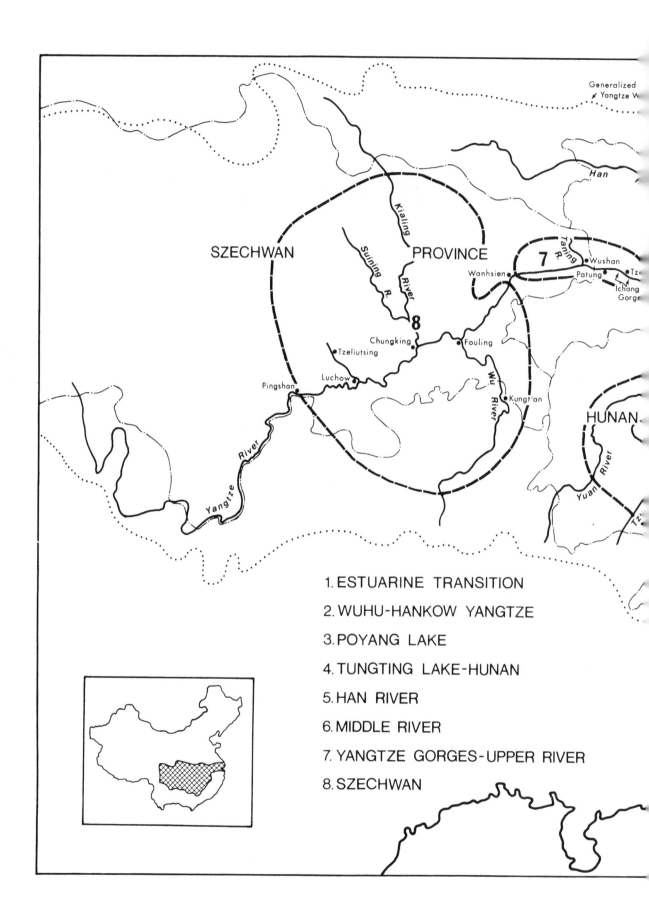

SZECHWAN PROVINCE

HUNAN

Generalized Yangtze W

Han

Kialing

Suining R.

River

Taning R.

7

Wushan

Wanhsien

Patung

Tze

Ichang Gorge

8

Chungking

Fouling

Tzeliutsing

Wu River

Luchow

Kungt'an

Pingshan

Yangtze River

Yuan River

Tz

1. ESTUARINE TRANSITION

2. WUHU-HANKOW YANGTZE

3. POYANG LAKE

4. TUNGTING LAKE-HUNAN

5. HAN RIVER

6. MIDDLE RIVER

7. YANGTZE GORGES-UPPER RIVER

8. SZECHWAN

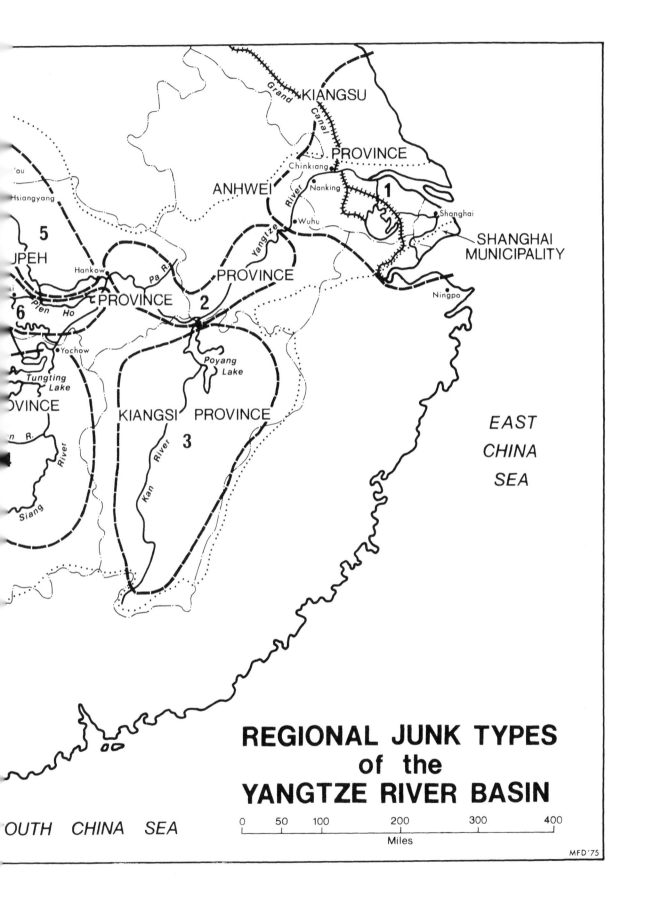

KIANGSU

Grand Canal

PROVINCE

Chinkiang

Nanking

ANHWEI

Yangtze River

Wuhu

1

Shanghai

SHANGHAI
MUNICIPALITY

'ou

Hsiangyang

5

JPEH

Hankow

Pa R.

PROVINCE

Ningpo

6

Pien Ho

PROVINCE

2

Yochow

Poyang
Lake

EAST

Tungting
Lake

CHINA

OVINCE

n R.

Siang

River

Kan River

KIANGSI PROVINCE

3

SEA

**REGIONAL JUNK TYPES
of the
YANGTZE RIVER BASIN**

| 0 | 50 | 100 | | 200 | 300 | 400 |

Miles

OUTH CHINA SEA

MFD'75

that a complete catalog of historic and modern boat types would run to at least 320 for the Yangtze Basin, grouped into about 40 to 50 different "families" of types. G. R. G. Worcester's summary listing includes specific comment on about 210 river junk styles, in addition to some coastwise craft, a variety of rafts, and other special water devices. As thorough as Worcester's listing (see Selective Bibliographic Notes) is for the lower Yangtze Basin, it is incomplete above Hankow on the Middle River, and the collection here presented includes several types Worcester omits.

A great many of the older types of watercraft have become extinct within the last century, and it is perhaps too late for accurately reconstructing the traditional water transportation system of the Yangtze Basin. Probably the total number of junks and sampans operating within and native to the Yangtze Basin approached 120,000 late in the nineteenth century when the first occidental river steamers began their serious entry into the river trade. I estimate that by about 1920 the number of junk types had been reduced to around 250, and that the total numbers of all craft were down to about 90,000. After 1930, the steam tug, the small steam launch, and the small river steamer began to multiply significantly, seriously disrupting the traditional system, and the total number of operating junks was on the verge of serious decline. One can only speculate that under Communist industrialization and modernization programs the variety and total number of such craft will continue to dwindle. In partial compensation, perhaps, it is likely that those modernization programs will include improvements in water control, involving the removal of some of the traditional impediments to navigation on those streams judged critical to modern transportation networks, making the traditional, specialized craft less necessary than formerly.

REGIONALISM IN JUNK STYLES

In the modern era of steam navigation, the Yangtze River has been divided into three parts. The Lower River extends from the Yangtze Delta's estuarine mouth to Hankow (Wuhan), a distance of six hundred miles, a section that is open to sea-going ships of moderate depth. The Middle River comprises the four-hundred-mile section from Hankow to Ichang, operable by river steamers. The Upper River historically often included everything above Ichang, but, for steam navigation, the term normally applies only to the four-hundred-mile section between Ichang and Chungking, a zone that still requires short but high-powered ships. Poyang Lake is normally classified as belonging to the Lower River, whereas Tungting Lake is part of the Middle River. Traditional Chinese categorization of the river has been more localized, dividing it into many more units that correspond to local conditions of navigation and regional trade flows.

Inland water junks must, first of all, be distinguished from the sea-going junks of the China coast, even though simple generalizations become somewhat inaccurate. River junks tend to be shallower and to have flatter bottoms; their proportions of length to beam are greater; they use different kinds of rudders, which are slung differently; they mount fewer sails, which are cut differently; and they never carry decorations on the hull. The largest of the inland craft tend to be smaller, with less cargo capacity, and they normally carry smaller crews. In exception to these generalizations, the coastal junks of North China tend to be flat-bottomed in response to the shallow waters of the margins of the Gulf of Pohai, whereas the junks of the Central and South China coasts are deep-bottomed with rounded hulls. And not all coastal craft are highly decorated.

The Estuarine Transition Zone

The 110-mile section of the Lower River between Chinkiang and Wuhu forms a transition zone in

A small junk on the Lower River near Nanking illustrates the shape of sail normally used on freshwater craft in the Yangtze Delta. New strips of sail cloth have replaced worn sections of the sail.

A fishing boat off the port of Shasi shows the shape of sail normally used on most craft in Central China waters. The sail has been patched by setting in new pieces of sail cloth, but the hole at lower left corner of the sail now needs mending.

riverine conditions and consequently in junk styles. Chinkiang is roughly at the head of the estuarine fill now forming the Yangtze Delta, and Wuhu is about 250 miles from the present mouth of the Yangtze. Within the transition zone tidal effects decrease toward Wuhu, the broad river narrows, channel crossings over shallows tend to be more stable, and the flow characteristics of the stream become more riverine. It is within this zone that river navigation becomes a more selective process than sailing on the broad open waters of the estuary or the China Sea. The use of leeboards becomes less frequent, and

fewer craft mount the sea-going drop-rudder; those junk types that retain both items tend to have their trading range downstream rather than upstream. The proportions of length to beam shift to those of the river rather than the coast. Coastal craft often are built on a proportion of four to four-and-a-half to one, whereas a proportion of five to five-and-a-half to one is more typical of riverine craft. Whatever their build, junks with home ports on this section of the river never carry decoration on the hull but are treated to several coats of tung oil like all other river

All Szechwan craft mounting sails employ the square sail rolled on a yard. The sail in the foreground still pulls well even though tattered, since the sail is made of vertical strips of cloth sewn, or roped, together.

Two large junks of the *Lao-Hua-Ch'iu* class are bound upstream on the Kialing River, Szechwan, each having a full crew of oarsmen and each mounting mat sails. The far junk has five mats mounted, the near one six. The model in the collection is shown with a cloth sail, but a few junks of this class still mounted mat sails in the 1930's.

craft. River craft use a balance rudder: the blade extends both fore and aft of the rudder post, unlike the sea-going junks, in which the rudder can be let down several feet when at sea. On river craft the length of the two parts of the blade and the depth of the blade are very closely related to the build of the specific junk.

Many of the craft of the transition zone are built with a poling gangway on either side, running the length of the junk, a feature never found on coastal craft. Although the poling gangway is not found on all inland craft, it is almost standard on lake craft. The coastal junks, at least in recent centuries, always have cabin housing of solid wood, sturdily built, whereas more lightly constructed housing and bamboo mat roofing are found on some transition zone junks, and mat roofing becomes the norm above Wuhu, even though a few inland junks use wood plank roofing. Large coastal junks normally mount from three to five sails. In the transition zone the number of sails may range from five to three, but no Wuhu junks or junks built higher up the river ever mount more than three sails. From Wuhu upriver all masts are stepped in the median line of the junk rather than scattered from port to starboard as in various of the coastal craft, and in river junks the masts seldom have a pronounced rake. Below Wuhu it is difficult to distinguish between riverine and sea-going junks by the cut of their sails, whereas a fairly uniformly cut lug sail is generally used between Wuhu, on the Lower River, and Wanhsien, on the Upper River.

Within the whole of the transition zone, there are nearly twenty different families of craft and at least seventy-five separate styles of junks in all. This excludes the Kiangsu and Ningpo sea-going craft working out of Shanghai and nearby ports. It does include all the junk types whose primary waters are fresh waters, both to the south and the north of Shanghai. Perhaps there were a few more styles operative in the days when the Grand Canal was a functioning water, before steamers replaced the salt junks working from central warehouses below Nanking and serving the Yangtze Valley as far upstream as Hankow. Except for the salt junks on the Yangtze and the grain tribute junks on the Grand Canal, almost all estuarine junk types were rather localized in their traffic patterns, seldom trading outside the sector below Nanking.

The Wuhu-Hankow Yangtze River Section

The stretch of river between Wuhu and Hankow is not notable for a wide variety of junk types. A few families of types are common to many of the river ports in this strip, but not more than fifteen distinctive styles originated here. This portion of the Yangtze is transit territory for the trading ranges of junks from higher up the river, or for junks out of Poyang Lake that range downriver to Shanghai or upriver to Hankow. Wuhu is the home port for three or four of these junk types, which trade the main river between Hankow and Shanghai. Smaller river ports in eastern Hupeh were, similarly, the home ports of only two or three junk styles that ranged the whole of the Lower River.

Poyang Lake

Most of the junks navigating Poyang Lake originated on one of several rivers that flow into the lake draining Kiangsi Province, although there were a few types that were distinctly lake boats only. Most Poyang Lake craft traded in a range that included either a river zone, the lake waters, and the Yangtze River down to Shanghai, or a river zone, the lake waters, and the Yangtze up to Hankow. A few of the distinctly lake traders seldom ventured beyond Kiukiang at the mouth of the lake channel. Many of the Poyang Lake craft were somewhat specialized in their cargo handling, which narrowed their trading ranges. The *Kan-Ch'uan* (see plate 1) is the only Poyang Lake junk style represented in the collection, since it was one of the few junks that traded to or ventured above Hankow. The model builder responsible for most of the models in the collection was not familiar with other Poyang Lake craft and did not offer to build any of them. Poyang Lake junk styles

Two yulohs and a bow steering sweep are being worked as a *Shou-K'ou Ma-Tang-Tzu* navigates a swirling patch of water over a reef in the gorges during a late spring rise.

are somewhat different from the styles of many regular river craft, and the region around Poyang Lake therefore constitutes a style region of its own, having six to eight families of junks with perhaps fifteen hybrid varieties evolved therefrom. Poyang Lake is gradually being filled with sediment by the streams flowing into it. During the summer it measures about twenty by ninety miles, but during the winter low-water period most of the lake surface is very shallow marsh and only the river channels through the lake-bed may be traveled. The coming of the powered tugboat, the steam launch, and the small steamer has been hard on the junk traffic of the whole Poyang Basin, and the older junk types were disappearing rapidly by the 1930's.

Tungting Lake–Hunan

Hunan Province, with many rivers flowing into Tungting Lake, has been one of the most productive sectors of the Yangtze Basin in the development of

Five oarsmen are here shown in working stance, propelling a small junk upstream against the current. Most crewmen wear hats much of the time, but often little else.

practical junk styles of superior design and excellent workmanship. There are both open-lake and river rapids-running craft in considerable variety. Some of both types were undoubtedly devised long before the settlement pattern became dominated by Chinese. Probably Tai and other non-Chinese ethnic stocks originated the boat-building traditions of Hunan. It is customary to say that all Chinese watercraft are descended from the ancient craft of North China, but this contradicts many aspects of the culture history of Central China, and I firmly believe that water navigation in at least the two lake provinces of Hunan and Hupeh preceded Chinese influence.

Out of a few basic families of prototypes of ancient lineage, Chinese boat builders in this region have, over the centuries, developed perhaps sixty or more specific types of junks in ten or twelve families. Each of the larger streams that flow into Tungting Lake is the home region for several types of craft ranging from those that navigate the lake and the lower reaches of the rivers to the specialized craft developed for the upper reaches. Hunan junk styles have been the models for many of the "new" junk types now only a few centuries old that are sufficiently adaptable to traffic widely on the different waters of the central Yangtze Basin. Many of the junk styles

in the collection are either Hunan styles or derivatives of Hunan styles. The practical serviceability of many Hunan junk styles permits a very wide trading range. Although the majority of junks travel between Hunan ports and Hankow, numbers of them travel downriver to Shanghai, and several Hunan junks are sturdy enough to travel through the Yangtze Gorges to Chungking. Hunan junks are very common all along the Middle River between Hankow and Ichang, often using one of the flood channels for access from Tungting Lake.

During the summer high-water period, Tungting Lake measures about sixty by seventy-five miles and the broad lake surface is largely navigable by shallow-water craft, but during the winter low-water period the lake is much smaller and quite irregular in outline and open water surface. In winter, in this century, many areas of shallow marsh are interlaced with narrow channels of water flowing from the river across the lakebed and out of the lake. Flood channels connect the Yangtze River, both west and east of Shasi, to the northern sector of the lake. These flood channels lessen the flood levels of the Middle River during freshets coming down the Upper River. Sediment brought down these flood channels is chiefly responsible for the greater amount of lake fill here than at Poyang Lake. There now are towns thirty miles from summer-level lake waters that were lake ports in the tenth century. The flood channels also form important navigation routes between Hunan and Hupeh trading territories.

The Han River

The Han River, as a tributary of the Yangtze, drains southernmost Shensi, parts of southwestern Honan, and northwestern Hupeh before joining the Yangtze at Hankow. Its upper course is navigable only by two or three kinds of small boats during the summer, but from Laohok'ou (Kwanghwa) the lower 330 miles is navigable by large junks the year around. This lower section crosses the main lowland of Hupeh Province, and here the Han lies above the plain, enclosed within an extensive dike system. The

The river front at Hsiangyang in northwest Hupeh on the Han River. The first two junks are variants of the *Ch'iu-Tzu* class. The near junk has its mast down and slung along the port side, yulohs and other gear are stacked on the lumber irons, and both junks have rolls of bamboo tracking line stacked on the decks. The near junk is riding empty; the second is almost fully loaded, riding deep in the water.

final few miles of the Han do not carry much water, since most of its flow drains off southward into the watery lowland between the Han and the Yangtze.

The lower Han River forms the home waters of several very old families of junks that have maintained their integrity right into modern times. In recent centuries Hunan craft have traded on the Han River also, and hybrid junk styles have developed, blending the two old traditions. There have been ten or twelve specific hybrid styles built in the towns along the river, with Laohok'ou and Hsiangyang being the most common home ports, near the upper end of the trading range. Several Hunan-style junks have also been built in various of these river towns, and in the nineteenth century there were about seventeen or eighteen different junk styles built and trading along the whole course of the Han. Many of the traditional junk types are worked by traders who largely confine their trading ranges to the Han River itself between Laohok'ou and Hankow.

The Middle River

In the Middle River unit of the Yangtze, from Ichang to Hankow, the river meanders over a broad, flat lowland, flowing just over 380 miles while dropping only 100 feet in covering an air-line distance of 200 miles. Under entirely natural conditions, the primary flow channels would undoubtedly shift periodically, but for centuries the river has been constrained by a complex multiple dike system. In the central zone the river lies well above the plain during the summer high-water season, and there are flood channels that are kept open to drain off some of the water into the surrounding lowlands. Despite the dike system and the flood channels, breaks in the dikes still do occur at long intervals, and much of the lowland then goes under water for one to three months. The chief flood channels, in recent centuries, have drained water southward into the Tungting Lake basin, but there is some escape to the north. The region north of the Yangtze, but south of the Han, has long been a watery maze of lakes and connecting channels that filter water eastward to points at which it can rejoin the Yangtze. It is not clear just how old the present channel known as the Pien Ho may be, but junk traffic has used it for centuries as a quiet shortcut between Hankow and Shasi. Periodic changes in the details of lakes and channels do occur, and since there are also seasonal changes, very few maps present the patterns effectively. This between-rivers hinterland, particularly, is a zone of difficult land transportation, and only in the modern period of road building have land routes begun to be at all competitive with water transportation.

Most of the junk styles found along the Middle River are derivative types chiefly hybridized from three or four ancient Hunan junk families. Depending on which criteria are applied, about twenty such hybrid styles are at home in this region today. As settlement has accumulated higher population densities in recent centuries, Shasi has become an important regional entrepôt, the volume of commodity movements has increased, and the operators of watercraft have developed various specialized trading systems and territorial ranges in which particular junk styles have been worked out. The region has become a zone of overlapping traffic patterns, with Szechwan, Hunan, and Hupeh junks working the main river downstream to Hankow and upstream to Ichang, and a variety of Shasi-based junks working the between-rivers hinterland zone and a local zone along the Yangtze.

The Yangtze Gorges–Upper River

Ichang is the break-point between the Middle River and the Upper River, and between two quite different kinds of river navigation, whether for native craft or for modern high-power steel vessels. The Yangtze Gorges dominate the Upper River, extending from a few miles above Ichang to just below Wanhsien, a distance of about 180 miles. In this section the great river follows a deep canyon across and through an enormous zone of folded-arch mountain ranges. Between Chungking and Ichang the river drops about 600 feet in somewhat under 400 miles, so there is a brisk current flowing all year long. Between Wanhsien and Ichang the river alternately flows through almost vertically walled narrow canyons of hard, ancient gneisses and limestones (the gorges) and the slightly more open sections of softer conglomerates, shales, and sandstones that have weathered and eroded into steep slopes along the river, sometimes cut by tributaries into narrow valleys. There are eight gorges ranging from four to thirty miles in length—deep-water narrows in which the height of the river may vary 200 feet from summer flood freshet between June and September to winter low-water between December and March. During the summer period a freshet sometimes provokes very turbulent currents through the gorges that may approach fourteen knots, and the river may rise or fall fifty feet in a day. Junk traffic traditionally ceased during the peak high-water season. During a freshet the gorges do become almost impassable to native craft, but at lesser river stages they can be navigated. The gorges in Szechwan have a trackers' path hewn out of the solid rock walls, but the Hupeh

A variant of the *Pa-Wan-Ch'uan* class of Kialing River junk is sailing upstream under a sail made of reed and bamboo matting. This is an old junk engaged in the coal trade down the Kialing; such junks in the 1930's still used matting sails. Stacked on the roof are other mats that can be mounted to increase the dimension of sail. The junk captain stands on a plank laid across an extension of the house planking, a very common feature in junks having a house amidships.

A variant of the *Tao-Pa-Tzu* class junk from the Lien River, a tributary of the Siang River of central Hunan, is a coal carrier on the downstream journey but a general cargo carrier on the upstream journey. It is one of the few Hunan junks that mount a sail lacking the markedly rounded shoulder on the high peak of the sail. The house is built of wood, but it normally carries a matting cover over the roof planking. Seen here, the junk is homeward bound from Hankow, carrying only a little cargo.

There is never a clear day in the Ichang Gorge, the first gorge above Ichang. This is the lower section of the fourteen-mile gorge at median water, and the river flows out of the distant mists.

A group of junks await cargo during a rainy spell at Ichang, with their mat covers keeping the decks dry as the spring rise covers the foreshore.

A *Shou-K'ou Ma-Yang-Tzu* class junk has been freshly oiled with tung oil and is laid up for the winter in a pool on the low-water foreshore at Ichang. The sail is stored on the deck, and a full set of mats, held in place by the poles hanging below, has been rigged to keep the deck dry.

The stern of a *Shou-K'ou Ma-Yang-Tzu* rises high out of the water. Laid up for the winter, this junk has had its rudder removed. The opening at the right is a garbage chute, and the central rectangle is a window in the captain's cabin termed the "swallow's door." The poles hanging alongside are part of the set of weighted material holding the rain-mats in place.

portion of this track never was completed and the trackers must make their way as best they can over the rock-strewn shore. These gangs of men, using split-and-braided bamboo cables up to 1,500 feet long, slowly and laboriously haul a junk up a rapid, or haul it upstream against a strong current. During summer periods the easterly breeze fails more often than not and more than normal tracking is needed, considerably adding to the expense of a summer journey. Cessation of traffic during the summer is thus more a matter of comparative costs than of sheer inability to get a junk through the gorges.

There are over seventy points at which a rapid may exist at some water stage less than flood, but a good many of these at mid-stage are caused by rock ledges projecting into the river and deflecting the flow of the current into narrow and fast races, not by rock-strewn shallows. At winter low-water stages there are about fifteen rapids of variable severity,

depending upon the precise level of the river. It is the latter group that cause the chief problems for river traffic, since surmounting a rapid involves a vertical lift through rock-strewn channels. Some rapids were caused by rock falls and slides, whereas others result from bottom reefs and ledges. Most rapids are between, or on the margins of, the gorges. At a given water stage ascending a rapid involves passage through a narrow opening in the face of an extra-swift current and a vertical lift of three to eight feet. Descending a rapid involves choosing a narrow passage through turbulent boils that may barely cover jagged rocks, below which whirlpools and eddies pose a second kind of hazard. The casualty rate has always been rather high in both directions. There are a few rapids above Wanhsien, scattered out to a point not far below Chungking, but none of these is as severe as several below Wanhsien. The rapids near Chungking are significant chiefly because they limit the downstream traffic of the craft whose home ports lie at or above Chungking.

Although there generally is a prevailing easterly breeze blowing up the gorges during the winter season, by which junks can often sail through, the rapids can be ascended only by literally hauling a junk up and over the lip of the rapid. The tracking gang sometimes numbers two hundred for a large and heavily laden junk at a rapid with a high lift and a swift current. Special pilots locally resident at each major rapid always handle a junk through a rapid on both the upbound and downbound trips. Stout craft are necessary for work on the Upper River, since the junks undergo considerable stress on the upward haul and both upbound and downbound craft take considerable battering from the current and the rocks of the rapids.

For the through-run journey with large freight loads, most of the satisfactory junk styles of the modern Upper River evolved out of the Hunan *Ma-Yang-Tzu* class, the most successful of which has been the *Shou-K'ou Ma-Yang-Tzu* (see plates 21 and 22). Since the original *Ma-Yang-Tzu* had been built to navigate rough-water rapids on the Yuan River, it proved a very suitable prototype for the few styles of junks developed in recent centuries to work the Upper River. A few other styles of Middle River craft have proved adequate to occasional trips through the arduous routine of Upper River travel, and a very few styles of junks at home above Chungking make a rare trip down to Ichang and back, but these latter are exceptional cases.

In relatively recent centuries several small junk styles have developed to serve local traffic needs on sections of the Upper River, both above and within the gorges. Within the last century two or three types of craft, such as the Postal Boat, have also been developed as hybrid styles to serve specialized needs along the Upper River. Beyond the traffic pattern on the big river itself, a number of navigable tributary streams present unique conditions of waters or channels, and several highly individualized junk styles

evolved long ago for service on those streams. The collection presents some of these, but there are a good many that have not been cataloged. Including the craft of the Yangtze itself, there must be at least thirty different styles of boats in about seven or eight family traditions at home on some waters between Ichang and Chungking. Some of these, within Szechwan Province, represent distinct Szechwan types with certain peculiar characteristics.

During World War II mechanical towing devices were installed at some of the most difficult rapids, and since that time public works projects have made some progress at clearing channels through the more difficult rapids. It may be that future development of this sort will significantly alter navigation problems on the Upper River. In the historic era of Upper River navigation no significant attempts were ever made, with limited technologies then available and attitudes of government then prevalent, to alter the basic conditions of navigation through the gorges, and solutions of those problems were left to boatmen. The solutions lay in the development of particularly stout junks, the perfection of pilot skills, and the maturing of the art of tracking. Junk styles suitable for long-distance, heavy-duty navigation on the Upper River became specialized ones not really suitable for traffic on other sections of the river.

Szechwan

The large western region that comprises Szechwan Province forms a rather separate regional grouping of junk styles, excluding the craft built for the run through the gorges. There has been little hybridization involving styles from outside the region. The name of the province is used to refer to four rivers, the Yangtze and its three large tributaries, the Kialing, the Lu, and the Min, from east to west. There are, however, several other rivers, or tributaries of one of the three, that are navigable in some degree. Chungking and Wanhsien have been among the more important centers of junk building in the Yangtze Basin, but many of the craft built at Chung-

Junks of Central China

A small *wupan* is being worked up the four-foot lift of a boulder-bar rapid on a little river in western Hupeh at medium low water. The second man of a two-man tracking team is visible at the far right, and two men are wading the rapid pushing the boat. The mast is propped at an angle, and the sail and a mat awning are spread across the mast as a sun shade.

king and most of those constructed at Wanhsien have served the Upper River through-run freight route connecting Szechwan with Hupeh river ports. Chungking has been the center for building many of the larger craft used on Szechwan waters, some of which traffic on all the larger provincial streams. There are a good many local centers of boat building, however, and many junk types restricted to particular streams are built at points along the home stream. Many of the smaller craft working middle and upper sections of provincial rivers never carry sails, and some of them are small enough that the term "small boat" is more applicable than the term "junk." Almost all Szechwan streams have rapids on their courses, and it is the particular characteristics of a set of rapids, depths of water, or the nature of the current flow that restrict junks to their home streams.

There are several distinctive features that set Szechwan junk styles apart from those of other sec-

tions of the Yangtze Basin. For craft mounting a sail, only one type is used, the square sail furled on a yard, illustrated in the collection by the *Lao-Hua-Ch'iu* (see plate 29). Many of the junks of the tributary streams are more crudely built than those of Hunan and Hupeh, particularly, and the *Wai-P'i-Ku* (see plate 28) is an example (though the model in the collection is too smoothly made). Often the house has almost no furnishings other than the ubiquitous stove. Finishing work and caulking of seams is adequate below the waterline but often slipshod above. Almost all Szechwan junks and small boats engaged in more than local port traffic employ the stick-in-the-mud anchor post, mounted either in the bow or the stern.

It would appear that the junk types of Szechwan developed for navigating provincial waters represent one general tradition of boat building within the Yangtze Basin. Many of these go far back in historic evolutionary pattern, but at the same time the craft seem also to represent a simpler, more slipshod, and more spartan tradition. Many small features of workmanship that time and experience have put into the styles of junks on the lower sections of the river have never been adopted on the Szechwan junks. Not that they do not show very particular features of build designed to solve problems of local navigation, but

the pride of craftsmanship has never been carried as far in the Szechwan junks as in, for example, the Hunan junks. In the province as a whole, including tributaries joining the Yangtze at Wushan or above, there must be at least sixty-five distinct styles of junk. Here my knowledge is insufficient to group the many styles into families, but it seems likely that about ten or twelve family traditions are represented.

NAVIGATION OF A CROOKED-STERN JUNK

Several of the junk styles of the Yangtze Basin have peculiar abnormalities that always intrigue the nautically minded. Twisted bows and crooked sterns show up on a number of types, and the boatmen today operating such craft can give only mythical or fanciful answers as to why such peculiar features are still built into all junks of that type. There always seems to be a sound navigational reason behind the abnormality, for the peculiar feature seems to solve some practical problem of successfully handling the junk on the waters for which it was built. Most of the abnormalities evolved a long time ago through trial-and-error construction. Successful features were copied as the style became traditionalized, but modern boatmen often are not really aware of the basic reasons for the feature, though it continues to be practical in handling the junk.

Worcester devoted considerable attention to the reasons for the crooked bow of the salt junks of Tzeliutsing in central Szechwan and described the pattern of navigation quite fully. He did not, however, travel on the most famous of the crooked junks, the *Wai-P'i-Ku* (see plate 28), and did not explain the water conditions that probably are responsible for the crooked stern. Since a model of this junk, though incorrect in some details, is included in the collection, an explanation of what I believe is the basis for the peculiar construction is presented here.

The Wu River, on all four lower sections of which the crooked-stern junk is used, has a great many miles

of vertical canyon walls, against which the current piles up turbulently when rounding bends. Some of its many rapids are double-stage affairs, with the current shifting from one side of the river to the other within a short distance. At certain water stages, many rapids have large whirlpools below them. Some of these whirlpools are very broad and have depressed centers with wave patterns breaking toward the vortex. Navigation often calls for abrupt changes of course on split-second timing, since river velocities range from three to fifteen knots on some reaches at particular water stages and a junk shooting a rapid may exceed fifteen knots for a brief interval. There are few sections of violent waters through which a junk can ride out the current smoothly on the downbound trip, and no junk equipped with only a full-balance rudder could navigate the river downbound.

On the upriver trip the straight reaches in the canyons can be rowed through at many water stages, since these junks mount no sail, and only the full flood stage makes the canyons difficult on the straight reaches. Junks travel upstream in groups, and the tracking crews combine to move one junk at a time up a rapid or around a difficult bend. The several tracking lines to each junk, together with crewmen on the bow handling poles by which to fend off the rocks, maintain a reasonable if precarious control over a junk. The upbound trip normally involves a good deal of tracking.

It is on the downstream journey that serious trouble may be encountered, for at the difficult points the junk is moving rapidly and often threatens to go out of control. This happened at one rapid to a junk on which I was a passenger. Since the large crooked-stern junks are specialized salt carriers on the upstream voyage, and since little cargo moves down the Wu, the big junks normally travel downstream almost empty. They then ride high in the water, and even a very large junk will thus have a short length at the waterline.

The secret of navigating the Wu River seems to relate to two primary requirements in steering control. First is the need to change course abruptly, across the flow of the current, while moving rapidly downstream, as at a turbulent canyon bend or in a double-stage rapid within which the water shifts sides. Second is the necessity to hold a course across a changing flow pattern against the swirling pressure of a vigorous whirlpool below a rapid. These needs do not appear on long straight reaches or in quiet waters, but both do emerge at the turbulent canyon bends and the double-stage rapids with whirlpools. The three steering sweeps on a crooked-stern junk provide extraordinary leverage by virtue of their great length. On a large junk with long sweeps, the bow sweep meets the water at from forty to fifty feet in front of the bow, and the main stern sweep makes water contact at from fifty to sixty feet off the stern. The junk captain's position atop the flying bridge enables him to watch the condition of the water close around the junk and to give commands both to the crewmen manning the bow sweep and to those manning the auxiliary stern sweep, so as to achieve action in unison with his own actions in handling the main stern sweep. The two main sweeps often suffice to spin the junk onto a new course within a few seconds. The auxiliary stern sweep is used only in very tight and precarious situations, and it seems to be there as an insurance feature.

In crossing a whirlpool, the two main sweeps will be held steady in the water and usually can hold a junk on a relatively straight course across a whirl-pool, even though that course is frequently a bumpy one. In some cases, here too, the auxiliary stern sweep may be used to provide extra leverage. The two stern sweeps, of course, may be worked at the same time, since the auxiliary sweep is mounted at a lower position, is shorter, and works under and within the point of water contact made by the main sweep. On my trip down the Wu the state of water was such that the two main sweeps provided adequate steering power on all the canyon bends and through all but one of the rapids.

Problems may arise in extraordinarily violent water, or when one sweep is accidentally disabled. This does happen, and it happened on my trip at a double-stage rapid with a whirlpool between the two stages. The junk had crossed the crooked tongue of the first stage of the rapid, but the whirlpool had widely spaced and high-breaking waves. The waves sent the junk into a series of violent pitching motions. As the stern rose high out of the water, the butt end of the main stern sweep slipped out of the hands of the captain and went high into the air to the limits of its control ropes. It then crashed down as the stern went down, knocking the captain off the flying bridge and down against the uprights to the bridge. On the next downward pitch of the stern, the sweep flew off its pivot bumkin into the river, breaking its control ropes. The captain had just given a command to the single steersman of the auxiliary sweep and it was in play when the main sweep failed, but this did not suffice and the junk spun crazily across the whirlpool, practically out of control. The junk went through the second stage of the rapid not quite broadside and very bumpily, having struck some rocks. In the course of going through the second stage of the rapid at the wrong angle, the blade of the stern sweep was snapped off and the tip end of the blade was broken off the bow sweep, so that the junk drifted downstream for some distance before it could be brought to a bank. It required most of a day with a jerry rig to hoist the big stern sweep back onto its bumkin and to repair the two broken sweeps. Interpreted by the mythological superstitions of the boatmen, the whole mishap had been my doing, since I had insisted on riding the voyage astride the cabin roof just in front of the flying bridge. From that perch, however, I had watched the exquisite timing of the main sweeps as they kept the junk under perfect control every time but one.

JUNK CONSTRUCTION

The early Chinese shipwrights undoubtedly experimented with a wide variety of woods in the very early development of Chinese watercraft. In that era forests were widespread and the variety of timber available must have been extensive. Qualities of particular timbers—durability, ease of working, and so on—certainly must have entered into the decisions as to what timbers were most satisfactory. In some manner the ship carpenters building particular types of junks finally settled on certain combinations of timbers as best for a particular junk type. That early pattern of wood usage became traditionalized, so that the wood used in construction became a part of the "style" of the various kinds of junks constructed. Just how much readjustment of timber types to junk types has taken place over the centuries is not at all clear. It remains true in the modern era, however, that a particular junk type seems always to be built of the woods traditionally associated with that type.

The tree cover of the Yangtze Basin no longer comprises extensive wild forests, although in the higher hill country and the mountains there are still many small and scattered stands of forest trees. All farmers and villagers tolerate the growth of tree seedlings almost everywhere in the landscape, and there is a conscious if minimal maintenance of saplings and young trees, since these will mature into salable products in time. Locally, there have been patterns of "reforestation," and there is a habit of tree planting in many parts of the rural countryside. Single trees reaching timber-productive size will be cut and marketed from many parts of the occupied landscape, so that there is a considerable flow of small lots of wood and timber to the dealers in timber, poles, lumber, and firewood. Dealers render

portions of their take into firewood, but many pieces that can be sold in the natural state are retained. Many purchasers of wood look for units in which the natural growth pattern will fit the usage intended, so that "grown-to-shape" pieces of timber are in demand.

The total tree cover of the Yangtze Basin still includes a great many genera, many of which are represented by large numbers of species. The region includes subtropical and mid-latitude, broadleaf and coniferous, hard- and softwood trees in very wide distributions. Some species range from the lowlands into the mountains; others are more restricted in their environmental tolerances and occur at particular elevations. Trees, to be economically valuable in China, need not be huge, and much of the annual wood harvest would not be considered ready for cutting in the United States. Since many of the tools and utensils, furniture, and other consumer items are produced and processed in the local handicraft operations typical of Chinese economy, raw wood is readily acceptable in smaller dimensions both by the dealers and by those who use wood products.

Chinese ship carpenters' reference to particular kinds of wood is rather casual much of the time, and a common language label very often applies to all related species rather than to one specific kind of wood, but this is also true elsewhere in the contemporary world. For example, thirty-two of the fifty-five species of oaks native to China grow within the Yangtze Basin, in particular distributions at different elevations. One species, *Quercus variabilis*, is widely distributed and persistent in the landscape. It is one of the preferred good timber producers and is widely used, but many other species are also har-

Five junks are slowly working upstream on the lower course of the Pa River, a north bank tributary of the Yangtze in eastern Hupeh. The junk at the right is an eastern Hupeh representative of the *Ya-Shao* class, the most common type in these waters. It is being tracked by one crewman on the path ahead of the junk.

vested and used. The Chinese linguistic term for oak covers all of them, in general use, and the term as used by ship carpenters rarely differentiates between different kinds of oak timbers. Although ship carpenters stay with the traditional types of wood in building a particular junk, there must be considerable latitude in the specific reference to a given variety of wood.

In broad generalization it probably is true that fir (often *Cunninghamia lanceolata*) is the most common timber used in building junks, since it is a relatively soft but tough wood that is fairly easily worked.

Cunninghamia is perhaps the most widely distributed single species in the Yangtze Basin below three thousand feet, and it is persistent in the landscape. There are other woods, however, that sometimes are used under the general label "fir." In the hill and mountain country of western Hupeh and eastern Szechwan, two species of cypress (*Cupressus* spp.) are very common and the Ichang, Wanhsien, and Chungking ship carpenters have long used both in junk construction, but there are a good many junipers that produce similar woods that pass under the heading of "cypress." Of the models presented in the collec-

An old Ichang lighter is canted on the winter foreshore for recaulking of the bottom seams. The deck planking has been removed, fully exposing the bulkheads.

The full-balance rudder of a *Shou-K'ou Ma-Yang-Tzu* is propped up on the Ichang foreshore. The bottom section of the rudder post shows the "grown to shape" choice of timber so often employed by Chinese ship carpenters.

An Ichang *T'o-Pien-Tzu* is loading stone at a quarry site in the Ichang Gorge and is about half loaded. The sails have been furled and covered with a waterproof mat.

Without a sail, this Ichang *T'o-Pien-Tzu* is being propelled by two yulohs worked by eight men each, as a crewman in the bow checks the depths with a sounding pole.

tion, most of the actual models are made of cypress, an easy-to-work wood readily available in Ichang, the home of the model builder.

In construction of a junk two kinds of wood are commonly used. In one type the bottom planks and the bulkheads may be built of fir and the sides of cypress, whereas in another type navigating the same waters the bottom planks will be built of cypress and the sides and bulkheads of fir. A third type used on the same waters may be entirely of fir. Laurel is used almost entirely in the bottom and side planking of junks built above Chungking, but the bulkheads always seem to be of fir. The large crooked-stern junk has bottom planking of either cedrela or one of the maples because the two woods will stand bending under wet heat without splitting or breaking; the bottom planking is always bent to form the lower part of the stern. The sides are usually built of the same wood as the bottom, but the bulkheads are always built of cypress.

All junks have a certain number of watertight bulkheads dividing the hold into separate compartments. If a relatively small number of bulkheads are built into a given junk type, there will be added a series of ribs against which to nail the side planking. Whenever possible junk carpenters try to make ribs from timber that was "grown to shape," so that the unit of wood will fit the curve from the bottom to the side with as little trimming and shaping as possible. Such "grown-to-shape" ribs are much stronger than straight timbers sawed to fit. For many of the fittings needed on junks, the builder will search for the "grown-to-shape" piece of timber that can be used.

In junk construction, ship carpenters normally work without plans, from memory on a rule-of-thumb basis, although the owner will have supplied a set of gross dimensions for the size of junk to be built. All members of a ship-carpenter crew work with the simplest of tools, quite few in number and rather crude by occidental standards. All members of the crew have in mind the "picture" of the particular style of junk they are building and, skilled at their

An Ichang *T'o-Pien-Tzu* is drifting slowly with the current below Ichang with a freeboard of about one foot. A steering sweep is now being used in the bow to give the unwieldy and heavily laden junk a bit more steerage power on the quiet waters of the Middle River.

trade, they produce it. No two examples come out precisely alike, owing to the rule-of-thumb operating procedure, but there is no mistaking the type when the builders are finished.

The planking to form the bottom of a junk will be laid out on the site and fastened together, with short planking scarfed onto any planking that is too short. Next the bulkheads will be put together and nailed onto the bottom. The sawmen, working with a string line and a saw, cut requested planks from raw logs just ahead of the carpenters. The hull planking is started against the bottom and built up on both sides at the same time, a windlass being used to pull the planks into place to give the hull the proper form. The ribs will be added as the side-planking is added, the sawmen continuing to cut requested pieces just ahead of the carpenters. Any heavy deck beams will be added when the sides have taken full shape. Deck planking and the house are added next. The various fittings, including the rudder shaped to the particular junk, are then added, completing the construction. Seams are caulked with a mixture of fiber, lime, and tung oil, and the junk will be given three coats of plain tung oil over a period of about two weeks while the sails and working gear are being built to order for the particular junk.

The Collection of Models

THE Texas A & M University collection of Chinese junk models presented in this volume represents a major nucleus of an original collection of about forty-five items representing twenty-eight junk types trading on Central China waterways. None of the models is to scale, but with few exceptions all are faithful relative models. Contact with one model builder and discussion about the making of models in general made me realize that the stock models made for the tourist trade often were finished in ways that would make them attractive to occidental tourists but also rendered them inaccurate. The model builder was engaged to make an accurate relative rendition of the *Shou-K'ou Ma-Yang-Tzu* (see plate 21). Comparison of that model with junks of its type on the river verified its accuracy. From that point on the one builder made all further models. It is with some confidence, then, that I can state that the collection as a whole is truly representative of the junk types of Hunan and Hupeh waters.

Of the total collection that was made, a fair number were duplicates, all of the *Shou-K'ou Ma-Yang-Tzu*. These were acquired with the intention of giving them to friends in the United States, and they were eventually given away. A few items we have retained, but with one exception they are duplicates of types represented in the collection. The collection therefore displays all the variety of different types that we felt we could provide.

There must be other collections of models of Chinese water craft scattered around the world, some in museums and some still in private hands, but to my knowledge this is the largest collection of freshwater junk types that has been made. There is one other large collection of Chinese watercraft, some twenty-seven items, in the British Science Museum, generally described in Worcester's *Sail and Sweep in China*. Of the items in that collection, however, fifteen are seagoing craft, three are rafts, one is a fictional ivory carving, and only eight represent freshwater craft of the Yangtze Basin. Of the eight, two are duplicated in the present collection, but in one case, the crooked-stern junk, the model in the collection is rather inaccurate in various details and was included only because it does show the general shape of the junk. The present collection of thirty-one items represents twenty-eight separate junk or sampan types, of which eleven were not mentioned at all by Worcester in *The Junks and Sampans of the Yangtze*, and two others that are named but for which no plans are presented.

Plates

KAN-CH'UAN

Most Poyang Lake craft were rather specialized and built for particular waters or particular trading circuits, and many did not often venture out onto the Yangtze River engaged in general cargo trade. The *Kan-Ch'uan*, however, was an exception to the pattern. As late as the end of the 1930's it could often be seen as far downriver as Nanking and as far upriver as Hankow, freighting rice, tea, and paper out of southern Kiangsi and hauling general cargo on the return journey. This model is the only Poyang Lake junk in the collection, but it is an elegant and stately craft when seen quietly sailing on smooth water with its sampan-tender in tow some distance off the stern. The coming of steam launches to Poyang Lake caused a marked decline in the junk traffic, and the specialized types have been disappearing rapidly. The *Kan-Ch'uan* may well endure longer than most because it is a general cargo carrier adaptable to changing conditions of river trade.

These junks are built on the large side, from 75 to 110 feet in length, with a beam of 14 to 25 feet but a depth of not more than 5.5 feet in the largest rendition. They load from 30 to 65 tons on 3 to 4 feet of water. There are shallows and rapids on the upper Kan River in southern Kiangsi where the junks are built, and the high bow, with its foredeck coaming, and the shallow depth reflect navigating conditions on the upper reaches. Two tall masts forward and aft of the cabin carry the sails in a slightly unusual position for a two-masted junk. The sails are of little use on much of the upper Kan River, however, and are then stored on the four lumber irons that are one of the distinctive features of a *Kan-Ch'uan*. (Known as "owl stands" in Chinese, the lumber irons are fixed frames or stanchions raised over the deck house which serve to store gear.) Other distinctive features are the high stern planking, the high roof over the tiller room, and the narrow covered passageway between the cabin and the tiller room. These several features make the *Kan-Ch'uan* one of the most easily recognized junk styles on the Yangtze River. Only a single pair of yulohs are generally carried, and these pivot on swing-out pivot beams. (Yulohs—anglicized from *yau-lu*, "sway oar"—are long, bent sculling oars that are roped to the deck at the end of the loom and worked over pivots by rowers in a standing position.) The cabin is built of solid wood with removable roof panels. The anchor is carried on a distinctive long cathead well out over the bow.

PLATE 1. Kan-Ch'uan

P'ING-T'IAO-TZU

From coal mines in southern Hunan the *P'ing-T'iao-Tzu* chiefly freights coal down the Tzu River into Tungting Lake and to Hankow, returning southbound with general cargo. Many junk styles show some rather peculiar feature of their build, often developed in response to particular criteria for collecting taxes at excise stations during imperial times. Whether the *P'ing-T'iao-Tzu* has its peculiar feature for this reason or whether it developed in some other way is not clear, but *ping-t'iao* means "long and narrow," and this junk has its greatest beam measurement well toward the stern (not fully and accurately executed in the model), just aft of the main cabin. These junks are very sturdily built, with several heavy wales running the length of the junk, the num-

ber depending on its length, and with extra bulkheads. The junk tapers slightly at the bow and markedly at the stern, which rises into a strong center post.

The *P'ing-T'iao-Tzu* are normally built from sixty to eighty feet in length, with a maximum beam (at the stern wide-point) of ten to twelve feet and a depth of four to five-and-a-half feet. They load from twenty to thirty-five tons of coal when bound downstream, riding deep in the water. A bow coaming protects the foredeck, a raised platform-coaming protects the forward cargo hold, and the afterdeck is raised above the level of the cabin deck. The house is built of matting as a single long cabin. The single mast is stepped far forward and is somewhat shorter than on many junks. The hull normally is built of cypress, except for the bottom planking, which is of fir.

PLATE 2. P'ing-T'iao-Tzu

WU-CHIANG-TZU

The small rendition of the *Wu-Chiang-Tzu* is one of the more shapely and cleanly built of all Central China craft. This junk style is among the more versatile, for, although it was originally built to trade on the shallow winter waters of Tungting Lake and the inland channels, larger versions have successfully navigated the Yangtze Gorges, and it used to be seen in both Wanhsien and Chungking, well out of home waters.

The smaller versions of this class, such as presented in the model, have a markedly upturned bow and a raised and slightly recurved stern, whereas on the larger craft both the bow and recurved stern may be several feet out of water, the stern then rising above the top of the rudder post. Both the bow and the stern may also flair outward slightly. The hull is thickened just below the level at which a wale might be placed, but the planking is worked smooth on an outward slant above and below this thickest point, presenting a smooth and clean line. A shallow-water rudder extends well out behind the stern, its curved top normally riding well out of water. The single mast of the smaller craft is stepped just forward of the midship point, aft of which a wood cabin with mat roofing is rather long for a small craft. Large versions mount two masts, with the smaller stepped well up in the bow. All *Wu-Chiang-Tzu* employ a stick-in-the-mud anchor post set just forward of the lift of the bow hull planking. Small craft can be worked by a two-man crew, but up to seven are needed on the largest junks of this class.

The *Wu-Chiang-Tzu* ranges from thirty-five to about sixty feet in length, from seven to ten feet of beam, and from a bare two to four feet in depth. Empty, the craft ride on eight to fifteen inches of water. The smaller *Wu-Chiang-Tzu* handle almost a two-ton cargo on about sixteen inches of water, riding fairly low in the waist with this load, but often they load little more than one ton and then draw a mere twelve inches. Large craft will handle four tons on about a two-and-a-half-foot draft. The shallow-draft characteristic makes the smaller versions of the *Wu-Chiang-Tzu* most useful craft on Tungting Lake at low water, when the narrow channels meander among the grass and reeds, the high bow then pushing its way through the narrow and overhung channels.

PLATE 3. Wu-Chiang-Tzu

MA-YANG PA-KAN

In the era before steam-powered vessels were introduced on Chinese waters, long-distance travel by boat was often the most convenient and comfortable form of transportation in the Yangtze Basin. There formerly were passenger variants of many different types of river and lake junks. Of course, the quality of accommodations depended upon one's financial or official status. Individuals and families of ordinary financial means often took cheap passage on regular freight junks, taking conditions as they came; perhaps one could equate this with the quality of steerage accommodations on occidental ocean steamships. Some freight junks were built with cabins large enough to carry a few passengers under slightly better conditions. The private individual of adequate means often chartered a junk for a specific trip. Regular passenger junks occasionally carried some cargo, but there were specific passenger quarters in large cabins built for the purpose. The well-to-do could bargain for commodious quarters on a regular passenger junk. High-ranking officials were provided specially equipped quarters on passenger junks or government junks that amounted to luxurious travel accommodations.

The moderately well-to-do traveling on Tungting Lake down to Hankow or up the Yuan River in Hunan could take passage on a *Ma-Yang Pa-Kan*, an upper-class passenger junk like the model; this would be the equivalent of first class or a luxury suite, depending on how much space on the *Pa-Kan* one paid for. Available in Hunan were *Pa-Kan* built on other basic-style hulls. The model appears to be

of a class that would carry some freight, since its forward deck has two hold sections. Some *Pa-Kan* were built with cabins forward of the mast and could not normally load cargo at all. Since cargo holds are present, the model obviously does not represent the sort of junk made available to a very high-ranking government official.

The *Ma-Yang Pa-Kan* had a hull constructed on the lines of the *Ma-Yang-Tzu* freight junk, but its bow and stern were constructed to higher levels, the bow to avoid splashing water and to part the reeds growing on some narrow channels of Tungting Lake and the lower reaches of the Yuan River, and the stern to provide a luxurious stern cabin. Four cross beams were retained in the construction, three of which serve as pivots for yulohs. On a junk primarily carrying passengers, a long bow steering boom was necessary to handle a vessel riding light in the water. A poling gangway was set outside the cabins and beyond the line of the hull of facilitate maneuvering in quiet shallow water. Cabin quarters were decorated with lattice designs often finished in red and black lacquer, and scrolls and wall hangings covered the insides of the cabins, in which ample good furniture was placed.

The *Ma-Yang Pa-Kan* ranged from 60 to 120 feet in length, had a wide beam of 14 to 22 feet, with a hull that was 4 to 5 feet deep only. Most *Pa-Kan* carried but one sail, stepped forward of the cabins, but large ones carried two sails, the foresail well up in the bow. The coming of steam power, in launches, tugs, and steamers, spelled the end of the passenger junks as such, and none have been in service since about 1910.

PLATE 4. Ma-Yang Pa-Kan

CHUNG-YEN-PAN

It is somewhat unusual that a new junk style could develop in the modern period, considering all the historic evolution of junk styles suited to the wide variety of old trade patterns. With the modern development of the Salt Revenue Administration after 1912, however, changed tax control procedures on salt distributed in northern Hunan produced new trading conditions, and a new junk style was one result of these changes. From Yochow, near the mouth of Tungting Lake, a wholesale trading region was established in northern Hunan throughout which salt was distributed by boat to minor wholesalers. New merchant trading rights were granted groups not already having fleets of junks, and the *Chung-Yen-Pan* resulted.

The *Chung-Yen-Pan* is a hybrid junk style, with features from older construction styles combined in different ways. A shallow and wide-beamed but angular turret-built hull was constructed with heavy timbering near the waterline without using wales, so that the upper hull slants inward, the timbers being given a smooth finish. A sturdy but clean-lined hull resulted, one that tapers slightly at both bow and stern. The heavy crossbeams of the *Ma-Yang-Tzu*

were incorporated, there being the bow-beam, three foredeck beams, and one near the stern, the latter appearing only as a bumkin on either side. A central cabin with wood sides and mat roof has its bottom planking continuing to the stern as a high coaming. The foredeck has only a very low coaming. A single mast is stepped just forward of the midship point, with the final foredeck crossbeam placed just forward of the mast to provide pivot points for two yulohs. The most distinctive feature of the new junk style was the use of laurel wood throughout, somewhat unusual in Middle Yangtze construction practice. Another feature was a set of waterproof mats, by which the whole junk could be fully protected from rain; although mat covers are provided for particular junk styles and some mat covering is available on almost all junks, a large cargo carrier is not often covered from stem to stern.

The *Chung-Yen-Pan* fleet was built to fairly uniform size, each junk being about seventy feet long, with a beam of about sixteen feet and holds of about four-and-a-half feet in depth. Often loaded with close to thirty tons of salt, the junks rode rather low in the water, counting on the relatively calm water conditions of the channels they normally worked.

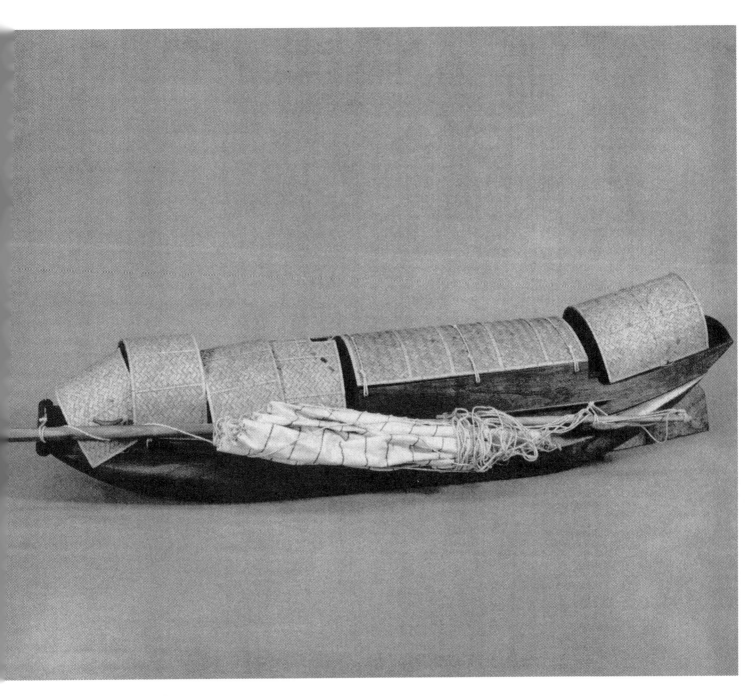

PLATE 5. Chung-Yen-Pan

CH'AN-TZU

Some junks were built for a rather specialized trade that both dictated their build and restricted their traffic routes. The *Ch'an-Tzu* was such a junk, built to carry salt from the government-controlled entrepôt and bulk-breaking point at Yochow, on the Yangtze River near the mouth of Tungting Lake, to a major wholesale distributing center at Shasi, up the Yangtze to the west. A fleet of *Ch'an-Tzu* was occupied in this particular trade for at least two hundred years, each junk making six to eight trips per year. Steamer transport of salt from coastal saltworks north of the mouth of the Yangtze began in the 1930's, and the existing *Ch'an-Tzu* were diverted to general cargo carriage on the middle Yangtze, but this specialized cargo carrier probably has no future in river transportation.

Built from fifty to sixty-five feet in length, with a beam of twelve to fourteen feet and a depth of four-and-a-half to five-and-a-half feet, the *Ch'an-Tzu* loaded twenty to thirty tons of salt at each trip, riding rather deeply in the water. As a specialized carrier of a product damaged by water, the *Ch'an-Tzu* had an unusual build. The mast was stepped far forward, and the space normally devoted to the crew's quarters in the main cabin formed part of the cargo space. A coaming protected the very short foredeck, under which there was no cargo hold. The first cargo hold, in front of the mast, was protected by a coaming with a platformed cover. The usual main cabin was replaced by a solid wood house roofed by solid wood removable panels, and cargo loading was done through this open space. A small cabin at the stern, roofed by matting, served to house the three- to four-man crew. The hull was always built of Cunninghamia fir and strengthened by four heavy wales running the length of the junk, since there were fewer bulkheads than normal. The cargo section within the main house had only one centrally placed bulkhead, to permit easier loading and unloading of the big and awkward split-bamboo baskets in which salt was shipped. The *Ch'an-Tzu* depended chiefly on its single sail for propulsion, but two yulohs could be pivoted on a removable crossbeam set between the mast and the cargo house, and a narrow poling gangway ran the length of the junk to allow maneuvering in shallow water.

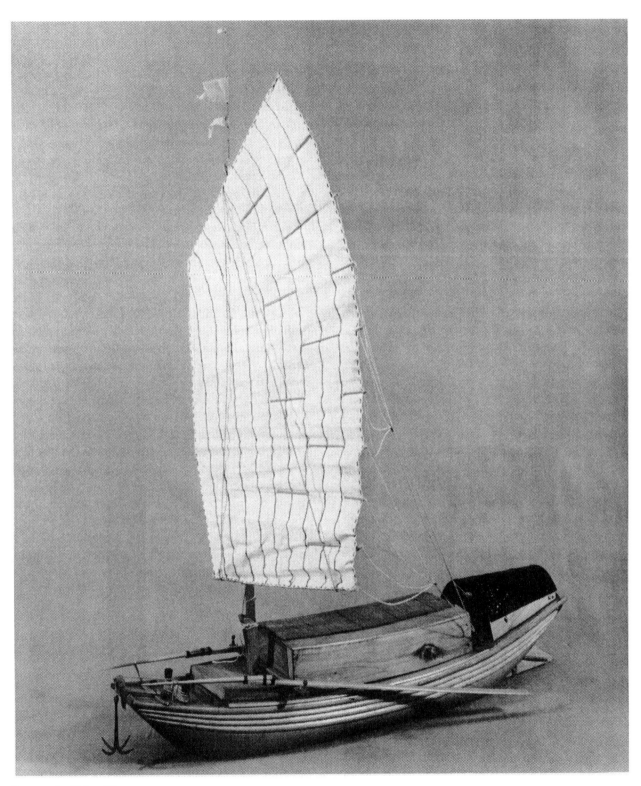

PLATE 6. Ch'an-Tzu

LAO-HO-K'OU CH'IU-TZU

The junk style known as the *Ch'iu-Tzu* is built at any one of several river ports on the middle Han River, two hundred to three hundred miles northwest of Hankow. Each river port finishes its craft in a slightly different way, but all boats possess the critical features establishing the class: the tapering bow and stern, the wood main cabin surmounted by three lumber irons, and the several wales along the hull, which serve as rubbing strakes. The model represents a Laohok'ou variant, in which the cabins are mat-roofed, the captain's cabin is built full width of the stern, the stern ends in a heavy high post, and the bow has a built-up and thickened coaming. Junks in this style from other home ports may have any one or more of several variant features, such as "bumper" timbers fitted over the bow in place of the thickened coaming, a second sail stepped well up in the bow, wood cabin roofs, even higher and recurved stern posts, and a narrower but solid-wood captain's cabin fitted with square ports having sliding closing boards.

The Han River and some of its navigable tributaries are relatively narrow waterways, but they formerly carried heavy junk traffic. The tapering bow and stern aid maneuvering in close quarters, and the rubbing strakes, the protected bow, and the heavy stern post are all protective features, since iron-shod quanting poles are used both for propulsion and for maneuvering the craft through crowded waters. Those respective portions of old junks long in service show the impact of being pushed about by the poles. Two stout crossbeams are fixed just forward and aft of the anchor capstan, and there is a third, removable when working cargo, located just forward of the cabin. These are used to hold the pivot points for the yulohs, which can be used in propulsion on the lower sections of the Han River. Yulohs are stored on the lumber irons when the junk is working the upper portions of the trading range, where it is propelled either by sail or by poling.

The Han River *Ch'iu-Tzu* do not have a wide trading range but confine their routes almost entirely to the Han River between Laohok'ou and Hankow, including the navigable portions of tributaries within this section of the river. There are difficult rapids on the upper Han, the first but a few miles above Laohok'ou, and the upper Han is quite shallow at low water; thus Laohok'ou is the head of navigation for all craft of the *Ch'iu-Tzu* class. These junks are built between fifty and seventy feet in length, and between ten and fifteen feet of beam, with a depth of four to five feet. All *Ch'iu-Tzu* are built of Cunninghamia, a native fir timber tree. The smaller craft handle up to twenty-five tons of general cargo on three feet of water, and the largest can load thirty-five tons on about the same draft. Since these craft have a tapering bow, making for difficult bow loading and unloading, all *Ch'iu-Tzu* carry a long heavy plank, stored on the lumber irons when the junk is under way, that is laid from a crossbeam to a shore point for the handling of cargo.

PLATE 7. Lao-Ho-K'ou Ch'iu-Tzu

HSIANG-YANG PIEN-TZU

Numerous hybrid junk styles combine particular features of two or more traditional classes; among these is the *Hsiang-yang Pien-Tzu*. Although many such craft list Hsiangyang, in northwest Hupeh, as home port, craft of this class in the 1930's operated out of a number of home ports along the middle and lower Han River and also along the Pien Ho to Shasi on the Yangtze River. Essentially, the *Hsiang-yang Pien-Tzu* is a broad-beamed, shallow-draft, general-purpose freight junk, amenable to handling under different seasonal water conditions year round on the Pien Ho and the Han River and its tributaries. The hull is built on the general lines of the traditional Hunan *Pien-Tzu* class, but the stern has a stronger sheer, giving the stern section a squat, full bottom. The wales on this junk serve as rubbing strakes. The main cabin is built of wood with a roof of removable roof boards, a feature derived from many of the Han River *Ch'iu-Tzu*, but the stern cabin was taken from the *Pien-Tzu*. Both these classes of junks, in the larger versions, mount two masts stepped well forward, and this is a characteristic of the *Hsiang-yang Pien-Tzu*. A poling gangway runs the length of the junk. A cathead fitted over the bow handles the anchor cable, and a removable crossbeam, notched into the forward washboard extension of the main cabin, holds the pivot pins for the two yulohs that may be used when navigating wider reaches of water.

Peculiar to the *Hsiang-yang Pien-Tzu* are the four bollards in the prow and the towing reel mounted on a platform over the stern. It is most likely that both form a rather modern addition, the purpose of which is to allow the towing of several *Pien-Tzu* by a steam launch on the lower Han River and, during high water, on sections of the Pien Ho.

The *Hsiang-yang Pien-Tzu* normally are built of Cunninghamia fir from forty to sixty feet in length, from seven to twelve feet in beam, and three-and-a-half to four feet in depth. As general cargo carriers, they load from about nine to fourteen tons cargo on two-and-a-half to three feet of water.

PLATE 8. Hsiang-yang Pien-Tzu

CHING-PANG HUA-TZU

The port of Shasi, near the western margin of the lake-and-canal country of Central China, is a crossroads entrepôt and the meeting port of many junk traffic patterns. It is also the home port of a number of varieties of junk, although some of those calling Shasi home port are actually built elsewhere. The general class of junk known as the *Ching-Pang Hua-Tzu* covers a wide range of specific craft whose home port is Shasi. These range from medium-sized freight junks loading up to thirty tons down to small inland watercraft with a capacity of about one ton. The larger variants are built about sixty feet in length, with a beam of about twelve feet and a depth of about four-and-a-half feet; carrying a thirty-ton cargo such a junk will draw about three feet of water. The accompanying model represents a large version of the *Ching-Pang Hua-Tzu*.

According to tradition, this junk type originated from a blending of a *Ma-Yang-Tzu* and a *Pien-Tzu*, producing a junk with the stout hull of the first and the broad beam and shallow draft of the latter. Both the *Ma-Yang-Tzu* and the *Pien-Tzu* were first built in Hunan, to the south, but the *Ching-Pang Hua-Tzu* is itself a very old craft. Historically, this junk type ranged a traffic zone that included the lower section of the Yangtze Gorges, the Middle Yangtze River, and Tungting Lake and its tributaries in Hunan.

A fairly high-riding deck, wales along the flanks of the hull, a single mast, a low double cabin amidships, and a poling gangway the length of the junk are the chief characteristics of the larger versions of the *Ching-Pang Hua-Tzu*. A small stern cabin is separated from the main cabin, but removable washboards allow the fending off of steamer wash or choppy water splash. Both cabins have wood sidewalls and removable mat roof covers. Since the junk works many small ports and local landings, the poling gangway is frequently in use to move the craft through shallow waters or when a breeze fails. With a crewman on each side of the craft using a long bamboo pole the junk can be moved about in tight spots or poled through slack shallow water at a fair rate of progress. The crewmen plant their poles from a bow point, walking the length of the junk as it moves forward under them, then returning to the bow for another pushing session.

The *Ching-Pang Hua-Tzu* is used in general trade, but it serves chiefly as a distributor working outward from Shasi as a wholesaling center.

PLATE 9. Ching-Pang Hua-Tzu

CHING-PANG HUA-TZU

Smaller variants of the original large *Ching-Pang Hua-Tzu* slowly evolved around Shasi, retaining the basic name but designed and built to work the carrying trade on the Pien Ho and other inland waterways and shallow lakes that lie between Shasi, the Han River to the north, and Hankow to the east. Some of these smaller craft also worked out of Shasi on the Yangtze itself, serving the small towns and villages along the main river. They ranged down to little craft of thirty-five feet in length, having a six-foot beam and riding when light on inches of water, with a carrying capacity of one to two tons of cargo. The wales flanking the hull have been reduced to one effective but symbolic element, the stern cabin is gone, and the poling gangway has given way to oars, but the essential features of a sturdy, broad, shallow hull, the center cabin, and the single mast still are present.

Most maps of Central China do not adequately represent the maze of canalized creeks and shallow lakes that still lie north of Shasi, particularly during the summer high-water season. This zone has been, historically, under active sedimentation and there is less permanent water now than there formerly was, although sedimentation is less heavy than in the marginal zone around Tungting Lake. There formerly was a considerable hinterland better served by water than by land transportation, and this region formed the traffic zone of the smaller *Ching-Pang Hua-Tzu*. Often operated by itinerant distributors and collectors of small lots of trade goods, these little junks covered a wide range of territory. Movable mat covers stacked on the cabin roof could cover the bow and stern quarters, and the sail could be furled and covered when the junk was working local creeks, using the oars for propulsion. The coming of motor roads in the very recent period may well cut into the traffic pattern of these craft, but it will perhaps be some time before roads fully replace waterways in this watery maze.

PLATE 10. Ching-Pang Hua-Tzu

CHING-PANG-CH'UAN

One of the more common junk styles on the Yangtze River between Hankow and Ichang is the *Ching-Pang-Ch'uan*, named after the local term for the Yangtze near Shasi. This style represents an early modification of the *Ma-Yang-Tzu* class of junk; the hull has the heavy wales running the length of the junk and the broad bow and stern. The stern does not, however, have the high rake of most *Ma-Yang-Tzu*; the line of the gunwale lifts steadily toward a straight stern standing well out of water. As is true of many Central China craft, a poling gangway extends the length of the hull, and there is a narrow catwalk across the stern.

Both the main and the stern cabin are built of wood, rather light in construction and roofed with matting. The long main cabin has at least one square port on each side, fitted with a pin-hinged wood closing panel, and there is a short coaming forward of the main cabin framed by a transverse plank to prevent sloshing water from entering the cabin. Sometimes movable washboards are set across the opening between the main and the stern cabin. The *Ching-Pang-Ch'uan* always carries two masts, the foremast stepped far up in the bow and the mainmast just forward of midship in the forepart of the main cabin, although sometimes the cabin is shortened to begin just aft of the mainmast. The model shows just one crossbeam notched onto the coaming forward of the main cabin, serving to hold the yuloh pivot points. The *Ching-Pang-Ch'uan* sometimes ventures through the gorges to Chungking, for which voyage two or three more crossbeams will be lashed down to the bulkheads across the forepart of the main deck, but for working the river below Ichang these normally are removed. A single lumber iron at the after end of the main cabin serves to store the yulohs. A pair of bollards in the bow and an anchor-cable cathead appear on many of the more modern versions of the *Ching-Pang-Ch'uan*, as shown on this model; these were not present on the earlier versions of this junk style, but just when their use became common is uncertain.

The *Ching-Pang-Ch'uan* often have been built at any one of several port towns just downriver from Ichang. The bottom planking has traditionally been Cunninghamia fir, the main hull and superstructure cypress. Normally built between fifty-five and seventy-five feet in length, with a slightly narrow beam of ten to fourteen feet, these craft are somewhat shallow, never having a depth of more than five feet in the large junk, and they tend to ride rather low in the water when loaded with cargoes of twenty to forty tons.

PLATE II. Ching-Pang-Ch'uan

PIEN-HO HUA-TZU

Working out of Shasi on the local inland waterways and along the Yangtze River itself to nearby
villages is a small boat operated as a retail trader. It
was often operated by the trader alone, but during
the 1930's he sometimes had a youngster with him
to take a turn at the forward oar, raise or lower the
sail, or tie up at local landings. Traders carried small
stocks of common necessities in baskets and boxes
stacked in the cabin. Mostly, such men tried to sell
for cash, but on occasion they bartered for small
amounts of local produce that were then disposed
of in Shasi. There were, in earlier decades and during the 1930's, a good many of these floating shops
that maintained regular circuits and did a small but
continuing business.

The *Pien-Ho Hua-Tzu* is built from thirty to
forty-five feet in length, with a beam of six to just
over eight feet and a depth of about eighteen inches
to two feet. Built of fir and normally having but
three internal bulkheads, the craft has two wales
that strengthen the hull and serve as rubbing strakes.
A coaming extends from the bow to the after end of
the small cabin. A small mast is stepped just forward

of the cabin, although on some local circuits this is
not always in place. A shallow-water rudder is normally fitted to the transom stern. An anchor is seldom carried, the craft being tied to shore by a painter
secured to a ring on the foredeck. The cabin, on occasion, is removed for handling very bulky cargo,
such as raw cotton, on the return trip. A stern awning is set on posts to provide the operator headroom
to work the oars. The general lines of the craft
strongly resemble the Ichang-Shasi sampan, and it
may well be a somewhat larger version of that small
boat, enlarged sufficiently to carry light cargo.

Although large enough to work some of the villages along the north bank of the Yangtze River
near Shasi, the *Pien-Ho Hua-Tzu* operates chiefly in
the interior north and east of Shasi and in the inland
waterways, small creeks, and summer-period lakes,
including the Pien Ho itself. Seldom carrying much
weight and riding on inches of water when light,
the craft can be maneuvered into the smallest of
creeks. It serves as a retail distributor of consumer
goods among the hamlets and scattered villages in a
region in which, formerly, there were very few roads
in the watery maze.

PLATE 12. Pien-Ho Hua-Tzu

T'O-PIEN-TZU

Hunan Province is the home region of a rather ancient class of junks known as the *Pien-Tzu*, literally translatable only as "boat" but generally interpreted as "flat boat," since the generic name came to be applied to a broad-beamed, shallow-water craft with few distinctive characteristics. In the centuries since the type originated, it has been built in a number of ports, and in some cases a few of the modern craft of this class have become hybrid styles. They are widely used on the lower sections of Hunan rivers, on Tungting Lake, and on the Yangtze between Ichang and Hankow, and are perhaps the most common single type of craft to be found on the Pien Ho. The specific junk style known as the *T'o-Pien-Tzu* refers to a *Pien-Tzu* class junk built at Ichang for traffic on the canals and channels between the Yangtze and the western reaches of Tungting Lake and on the Pien Ho and other channels in the hinterland of Shasi between the Han River, the Yangtze River, and Hankow.

The Ichang-built *T'o-Pien-Tzu* incorporated two features from the *Ma-Yang-Tzu* class junks: the heavy crossbeam built into the bow and the sturdy wales along the hull. Because of the latter feature, fewer bulkheads are set within the hull than in many junks. One or two other crossbeams are sometimes laid across the junk, notched into the coaming that runs from the bow to the main mast. These are removable when cargo is loaded and serve chiefly to hold the fulcrum points for yulohs when the junk is traveling waters wide enough for yulohs to be employed at all. A poling gangway extends aft of the main mast right to the stern, and the junk is poled in very shallow water or in narrow channels at low water. All *Pien-Tzu* class junks mount two masts, the main mast very tall and stepped just forward of the midship point, and a smaller mast stepped well into the bow. Two small cabins at the stern provide only restricted quarters. The *T'o-Pien-Tzu* are normally built from forty to sixty-five feet in length, with a nine- to eleven-foot beam, and seldom are deeper than three-and-a-half feet. Smaller craft can load close to two tons and ride on about fifteen inches of water, whereas the large junks handle up to about ten tons, riding on two-and-a-half feet of water.

Some old *T'o-Pien-Tzu* of the larger sizes sometimes are converted into stone carriers, freighting building stone from a few miles above Ichang as far downriver as Hankow. When converted to this use, the larger craft will handle up to almost twenty tons of stone, but the junk then rides almost awash, with only a very few inches of freeboard. That they consistently load this heavily proves the practice is practical.

PLATE 13. T'o-Pien-Tzu

SHUI-PAO-CHIA FEI-HSIEH

Military watercraft date from a very early period in China. At least in the Yangtze Valley, military and police craft have had an important role in the changing political controls over the territories that today make up several of the provinces of Central China. What appears to be the last epoch of such craft under the Empire dated from the end of the Taiping Rebellion in 1865. In the Yangtze Valley a fleet of river police junks was active from that time until the end of the Empire in 1911. In 1892 the river police service was reorganized and given more explicit preventive duties with regard to the evasion of customs charges on craft engaged in internal river trade. These police junks were built in various sizes and styles according to the nature of the waters they were required to patrol.

The Hunan-Hupeh craft, generally broad-beamed, shallow-water junks equipped with a shallow-water rudder and an Ichang-type sail and mounting ten oars, were of a class known as the *Fei-Hsieh*, or Fast Crabs. They normally carried a crew of twelve, the ten oarsmen-police, a helmsman, and the captain. The single tall mast was stepped slightly forward of midship, and six oars were placed aft of the mast and four toward the bow. A poling gangway lay flush with the deck built outside the line of the hull. A small cabin at the stern housed the captain and the galley was in a shallow hold box just forward of the mast, protected by a coaming on either flank. When the junk lay at anchor, a cloth awning was slung over a bamboo pole resting on the cabin top and secured to the mast to cover the galley and crew sleeping quarters amidships. Bollards toward the bow served hawsers used to tie up to other craft or to a shore stake, since the one small cannon was mounted in the bow, displacing the anchor point. Various traditional weapons, still in use after 1892, were housed in holes in the poling gangway at the stern on either side of the captain's cabin.

From 1892 to 1911, Ichang was the base-port for a squadron of junks belonging to the river police, or *Shui-Pao-Chia*. The Ichang district included the Hupeh section of the Yangtze Gorges on the west and the port of Shasi on the east, but the craft seldom ventured beyond the foot the Ichang (Lampshine) Gorge. The junks of at least the Ichang squadron were built about forty feet long, with a hull beam of about nine feet, and were no deeper than two-and-a-half feet, riding on about ten inches of water. The model has a sail of the proper shape and height but improper in its makeup, since apparently all police junks mounted a sail made of alternate strips of blue and white cloth. The awning mounted amidships was also of alternate strips of blue and white cloth. The fleet of river police junks went out of operation in 1911, and nothing ever took its place, so this variety of watercraft became extinct with the demise of the Empire.

PLATE 14. Shui-Pao-Chia Fei-Hsieh

FAN-KUAN-CH'UAN

What happens to large junks that grow old in service without being wrecked? Some of them get turned into floating restaurants, tea houses, houseboats, or inns. Before they become unserviceable as cargo carriers, of course, many older junks get demoted from their regular traffic patterns to the carrying of stone, reeds, refuse-fertilizer, or other low-class service. The ports of China have numerous "decommissioned" junks converted into commercial service uses. Almost any elderly junk of almost any style, provided it is a large one with a still-sound hull, can be converted into a facility serving the floating traffic within a port. Restaurants and tea houses are the most common, particularly at those ports where passenger ships must anchor in the stream or out away from wharves and docks in the harbors. Any sizable port will have from three to four to a dozen of them, dependent upon the volume of steamer traffic.

The model shown is represented as converted into a restaurant or tea house from some craft of the *Ma-Yang-Tzu* class, broad-beamed, square-bowed, with heavy wales along the hull. The crossbeams have been removed, the deck has been cut back to its broadest point and rebuilt, a pair of bollards and an anchor capstan have been installed, and a house has been built most of the length of the junk. Some-times the house is built projecting over the sides of the hull to afford extra width, and at other times it is built out over the stern. The bow end of the house is fitted with closing boards that can be removed to leave the entrance wide open for customer access. Several tables and stools occupy the forepart of the house, and toward the stern will be a large water jar, a cookstove, a work-serving table, and kitchen cabinets. If the house has been projected over the stern, the sternmost section normally becomes living space for the operator of the establishment. The floating restaurant or tea house is a cumbersome craft and maneuvers slowly and awkwardly around a port.

At Ichang, where steamers had to anchor in the stream, the floating restaurant or tea house used to be tied up either to the shore or to the stern of some freight junk at a point somewhat above the normal steamer anchorage zone. As a steamer came into port, the floating restaurant put out into the stream using oars and/or yulohs, or poling in low water, floated down, caught on, and tied up at the stern of the steamer, from which point the deck passengers and others could easily be served. When the steamer left, the restaurant cast off, floated off downstream, painfully working its way back to the shore fringe, to haul back to its regular position by poling or boat-hooking its way along the craft tied up along the shore.

PLATE 15. Fan-Kuan-Ch'uan

I-CHANG PO-CH'UAN

The cargo lighter is strictly a utilitarian port craft developed after the coming of the keel-built ships of the Occident, since at most Chinese ports such ships anchor well out in deep water. Lighters of slightly different build are to be found in every port of China at which steamships call in the modern period. All cargo lighters are simply strongly constructed floating boxes designed to transfer cargo from ships to shore and vice versa.

The *I-Chang Po-Ch'uan* (literally, "transfer boat") is normally built about eighty feet long, with a fifteen-foot beam, and is just over four feet deep, to carry almost sixty tons. Old junks are never converted into cargo lighters. Ichang lighters must work against shallow water on the foreshore in fall and spring seasons; in winter the water drops below the foreshore shallows. Shanghai lighters are about sixty by fifteen by seven feet to handle sixty tons, and the big Hankow lighters run seventy-five by eighteen by seven feet to handle over a hundred tons.

Very heavily planked, with three full-length wales and fifteen bulkheads (seven of which are often covered by deck planking), the Ichang cargo lighter is an ungainly and awkward craft in the water. All lighters are equipped with rudders, but the Ichang lighter, facing a current that often runs swiftly, has a full-balance rudder set in a transom stern. Two strong bollards at the bow permit tying up and towing. Between the first and second bulkheads is an opening to the coffer-dam for pumping out the bilge, since on lighters the bulkheads are purposely not made watertight; deck planking splits, rain leaks into the bilge, and pumping is more easily done when each bulkhead chamber does not have to be pumped separately.

PLATE 16. I-Chang Po-Ch'uan

I-CHANG HUA-TZU

The Ichang sampan is a highly maneuverable *Hua-Tzu*, or small boat, developed to serve a river port with a swift-flowing stream, no dock space, and no slack water anchorage. The sampan works the shore waters among the tied-up junks, ferries passengers between anchored ships and shore, serves as a cross-river passenger ferry, and meets freight junks and river steamers out in the swift deep water. In shore waters and in regular ferry work a sampan can be handled by a single crewman working the long stern oars, but for meeting steamers two persons are needed. Men, women, and children operate sampans in shore waters, but cross-river work and meeting steamers require adult skill and strength. Lacking dock space, all steamers at Ichang must anchor well out in the stream, where the current is swift much of the year, since the north bank foreshore below the town is shallow and becomes exposed during winter low water.

Most Ichang sampans are built between twenty and thirty feet long, have a six-foot beam, taper slightly both fore and aft, and ride only inches deep in the water. Most are built of cypress, a light-colored wood, but a few are built of laurel, which turns deep brown when treated with tung oil. A flush foredeck has but a narrow coaming, and the after section has a shallow hold which is divided by one or two bulkheads topped by plank seats and is floored. The stern hold is always permanently covered by a standing mat awning set on posts, to permit the operator to work his oars standing, as all sampan people do. All Ichang sampans have transom sterns. The stern bulkhead is slotted to take a rudder, but the rudder is normally actively used only in shorewater working. Simply and soundly constructed, the Ichang sampan has few peculiar features of build, yet it is unlike any other river sampan. Its zone of use extends from a few miles above Ichang to a few miles below Shasi, including many of the local inland waterways just north of Shasi.

In meeting a steamer or a big junk coming into port, one crewman handles a bow oar, a bamboo boathook, and a short painter secured to a ring in the bow deck with a hook on its other end. The two long stern oars provide both propulsion and steering control. A sampan moves out from the shore downstream across the current until it is very close to the steamer or junk; at this point the bow crewman releases his oar and catches any possible hold with his boathook. In a critically timed maneuver, the stern oarsman then brings the boat about, and with a jolting lurch the sampan is in tow by the craft being met. A fleet of sampans make the approach to a passenger steamer, with several following boats temporarily hooking onto the first arrival. Once the steamer drops anchor the boats juggle their positions alongside, tying onto the steamer by the short bow painter. Skillful as experienced boatmen are, meeting a ship under full speed in a swift current involves frequent casualties among sampan crews and also among passengers trying to disembark onto the deck of a bobbing small boat before the ship drops anchor.

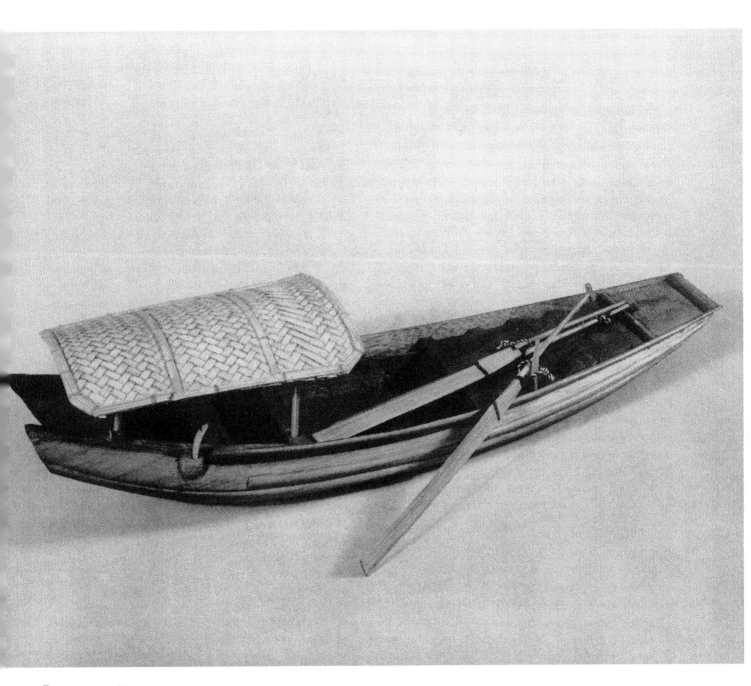

PLATE 17. I-Chang Hua-Tzu

I-CHANG LUNG-CH'UAN

The Dragon Boat Festival was one of the most important historic holidays in the traditional calendar of Chinese life. On the fifth day of the fifth month in the fourth century B.C., a poet statesman, Ch'u Yuan, committed suicide by drowning himself in Tungting Lake after being degraded by his ruler, Prince H'uai of the state of Ch'u, in what today forms the provinces of Hupeh and Hunan. A sonnet composed by Ch'u Yuan before the event later aroused his countrymen, who searched for his body with a fleet of boats. By stages the annual search turned into a national festival celebrated by picnics and by boating events in those localities having sufficient water to float boats. Many elements of animism and folk religion become associated with the festival, including a boat race in honor of Lung Wang, the Dragon King in the cult system of the river gods. The Dragon Boat, or *Lung-Ch'uan*, is the specially built boat used, with anywhere from two to twenty-five boats participating. A well-built boat may be preserved from year to year, but, by custom, one special boat is always broken up and burned as a ceremonial offering to Lung Wang. Feelings often run high between rival crews and their supporters, and sometimes small riots occur, so the races have been discouraged by modern government. Ichang had a history of relatively peaceful competition and was annually holding the races during the 1930's when my family and I were resident there. Races were run over a course about a mile long, heading downstream in the foreshore shallows on the north bank below the town, and witnessed by thousands of onlookers.

A *Lung-Ch'uan* could be built in any paired-unit dimension from 44 feet 4 inches to 110 feet 10 inches, although most boats were built 55 feet 5 inches or 66 feet 6 inches in length. The beam was about 3.5 feet, and the depth at the waist about 18 inches to 2 feet. A long, dressed-down fir pole was attached to an oak bottom plank, the bulkheads were slotted onto the pole, and three fir planks were warped onto the bulkheads to form each side of the hull. A second pole was slotted onto the tops of the bulkheads and capped by a line of planking to form a gangway. Woven bamboo rope was passed over the top of the planking and under the prow and the stern, to be tightened by twisting, amidships, to lift the prow and the stern slightly. Small platforms were built for the coxswain, the flagbearer, the drummer, and other such personages. The head and tail of the dragon were inserted into the bottom pole at the prow and the stern. The hull was gaudily painted to simulate the body of a dragon. Boatmen of each crew wore different colors, of symbolic significance.

A fifty-five-foot boat would have thirty-six paddlers seated in pairs on the eighteen bulkheads. The model is symbolic rather than to scale, with too few bulkheads and pairs of paddlers. Since this was a festive occasion in which pickup crews never practiced, the races were noted more for their antics than for form and speed, and all competing boats normally won prizes. A loaded boat usually had less than three inches of freeboard, water got shipped, accidents happened, and the race was more a spectacle than a competition. Ichang was notable, however, for a fairly legitimate operation, and its boats were often among the best made of those of any locality in the Yangtze Basin.

PLATE 18. I-Chang Lung-Ch'uan

WU-PAN

On the Yangtze River above Hankow the designation *Wu-Pan* signifies an open junk equipped with a sail and a stern steering sweep. Whereas the term *sampan* (literally, "three-board bottom") indicates any small boat used in fishing, ferrying, and in-port local usage, the term *wupan* (literally, "five-board bottom") indicates a larger craft used in interport traffic and open river work.

The *Wu-Pan* actually serves as an all-purpose, medium-sized junk on the river from Hankow as far upstream as Chungking. It is built in ranges from forty to sixty-five feet in length, with a beam of six to eight-and-a-half feet, a depth of three to four feet, with an open center hold eighteen to twenty inches deep. Rather lightly built, with a hull strengthened by wales the length of the junk, the *Wu-Pan* is light in the water and extremely maneuverable when lightly loaded. The *Wu-Pan* carries a rather large sail and, depending on the intended use, can be equipped with either yulohs or oars. Its stern steering boom normally is almost as long as the junk itself.

The *Wu-Pan* served during an earlier era as a fast small-cargo handler or as an urgent message carrier between Ichang and Chungking; with a full complement of eighteen oars and catching good summer breezes, the craft often made Chungking in twenty days. Long used in the gorges as a junk fleet-tender at a rapid, ferrying trackers and line between junks and shores, this craft, with a full complement of oarsmen, is highly maneuverable in rough waters. Dependent upon its size, the *Wu-Pan* handles from one to about five tons of compact cargo. Around Ichang the *Wu-Pan* has been used as a local interport trader, with the oars normally replaced by two to four yulohs. This particular model was built after a photograph of a *Wu-Pan* employed in the Ichang-Shasi local trade.

PLATE 19. Wu-Pan

YU-CHENG-CH'UAN

The *Yu-Cheng-Ch'uan*, or Postal Boat, is a modern development in China, and the model displays a hybrid junk style developed for service on the upper Yangtze River between Ichang and Chungking. The Postal Boat operated in both directions through the Yangtze Gorges, serving all the villages, towns, and cities along the river. For maneuverability in shallow village-port waters and for sturdiness through the rapids, a new hybrid style was developed. The new junk combined the heavy bow, strong crossbeams, and wales along the hull of the *Ma-Yang-Tzu*, the broad shallow build and the single, large Ichang-style sail of the *Wu-Pan*, and the transom stern, shallow-water rudder, and oars of the Ichang sampan. The sail was stepped amidships but was normally slung on the side of the craft on a downstream journey. Just aft of the mast was a solid wood cabin, on the panels of which were the large characters (reading from right to left) *Yu Cheng Ch'uan*. The bow was equipped to take a steering boom, which was used on the section between Ichang and Wanhsien. Uniformly built about forty feet long, with a beam of about seven feet just aft of the bow and tapering slightly toward the stern, and a hold about four feet deep, the Postal Boat was a very satisfactory junk style.

The Chinese imperial government traditionally had maintained a nationwide courier service for the dispatch of documents and the transport of officials, but all private mail was handled by a variety of private forwarding agencies. The imperial government allowed local officials to administer trade through the coastal ports, which resulted in unequal treatment at different ports. As European traders began contact with China, demand for uniform controls arose, and eventual treaty arrangements provided for a Maritime Customs to be established in 1861. Its longtime inspector general, Robert Hart, also envisioned the establishment of a nationwide postal service and, finally, in 1896, the Maritime Customs, having had the plans for the operation, was authorized to initiate such service. The Chinese Imperial Post Office was administered by the Maritime Customs until 1911, when a separate Postal Administration was created. In several riverine lowland parts of China, some routes operated on water for which existing junk styles were adequate. The difficult route to Szechwan through the Yangtze Gorges was another matter, however, and it was for this particular route that the new junk was built, since steamers did not then operate above Ichang.

The new route began operating in 1897, but no existing junk style was adequate to all problems faced. The new-style junks began operating in 1899, and within a few years there were between fifty and sixty in service on the Upper River, working out of Ichang, Wanhsien, and Chungking. The fleet was maintained at full strength into the late 1920's. A small steam launch made it to Chungking in 1898, but it had to be tracked over several rapids; in the following years, few other steam craft made the trip. It was 1926 before regular steamer traffic began on the Upper River, and rather quickly the Post Office began shipping mail to Wanshien and Chungking by steamer. The advent of steamer mail ended the use of the *Yu-Cheng-Ch'uan* on the through run. The Postal Boats operated on local runs for a few years, but by the mid-1930's other procedures had been devised to handle mail, and the *Yu-Cheng-Ch'uan* disappeared from the Yangtze.

PLATE 20. Yu-Cheng-Ch'uan

SHOU-K'OU MA-YANG-TZU

Within recent centuries this junk has been the workhorse of the shipping fleet on the Upper Yangtze River. Its traffic range has been from Shasi, in central western Hupeh, to Luchou, in southern Szechwan, but its home waters pour through the Yangtze Gorges between Chungking and Ichang. The prototype junk style, *Ma-Yang-Tzu*, originated many centuries ago in the town of Mayang on the Yuan River in western Hunan, where a stoutly built type of freight junk was devised to navigate the numerous rapids on that river. This specific type appears to have been built a few centuries ago in Chungking, given added strength and durability against the battering it receives in navigating the dangerous rocky rapids of the Yangtze in the gorges section. Since its derivation, this most practical and durable version of the traditional class of *Ma-Yang-Tzu* watercraft has been built in, and worked from, every significant port between Ichang and Chungking, although the largest numbers probably have been built at Wanhsien and Chungking. The *Shou-K'ou Ma-Yang-Tzu* has been popularly known as the *Pai-Mu-Ch'uan*, after the blonde cypress wood of which it is built, *pai-mu* being the term for "cypress."

The distinctive feature of the *Shou-K'ou Ma-Yang-Tzu* is the rounded barrel-build of the hull, which curves back inward well above the water line to narrow the width of the exposed deck surface. The narrowed deck surface rides higher than in many river junks, providing better protection from the splashing water encountered in the rapids. The turret-build, crossbeams, and three heavy wales running the length of the junk make for a very stout hull. The strong crossbeams built into the superstructure are characteristic of all *Ma-Yang-Tzu* class junks, but in this particular type they are exceptionally heavy, and the two on the quarter appear on either side only as bumkins. Besides providing hull strength they serve to secure the inbound ends of the tracking lines used to haul the junks upstream and over rapids.

The *Shou-K'ou Ma-Yang-Tzu* has been built in sizes ranging from 40 to 150 feet in length, although since the coming of steamship traffic on the Upper Yangtze they seldom are built longer than 110 feet. A freight junk of the latter length would run 19 to 20 feet of beam, have a hold depth of about 8.5 feet, and carry about 100 tons of cargo on about 5.5 feet of water. The basic style remains faithful regardless of the size of the junk constructed, although in different home ports the number of crossbeams varies and there are different patterns of fitting out the stern cabin belonging to the junk captain. A garbage chute appears on some junks, and some also have a rear port. Newly built junks are fitted out with ladders carried atop the cabins, but few old junks retain these. All junks of this class are fitted with three masts when newly built, but old junks seldom mount more than the foresail and mainsail. Cabin roofs, during the trip through the gorges, normally carry piles of plaited bamboo tracking line and soon turn almost black in color.

PLATE 21. Shou-K'ou Ma-Yang-Tzu

SHOU-K'OU MA-YANG-TZU

Comparison of this model with the previous one will disclose only minor structural differences. The finish differs, however, as decoration has been applied here. The *Shou-K'ou Ma-Yang-Tzu* is always built of light-colored cypress wood and treated with several coats of tung oil. A new junk, therefore, has a glistening blonde appearance, and the bamboo matting roofs are light-colored. Over the years, as successive coats of tung oil are applied right over the dust and dirt grimed into the finish, the color turns darker and darker until the wood becomes a dull gray-brown and the mat covers turn almost black. Occasionally a junk from some particular port may have its new ladders, ports, doors, and mast partners decorated in simple designs in red or black lacquer, but occidental-style paints are never applied to river junks. The Ichang model builders, however, catering to tourist interests, took to decorating parts of the models with foreign paints. As the model builder who built most of the models in this collection explained, tourists, having seen the highly decorated sea-going junks, often objected to the plainness of the Ichang models, so decoration to suit a buyer's fancy often was applied.

Notable features of the *Shou-K'ou Ma-Yang-Tzu* are the long yulohs that take the place of oars. These often are up to thirty-five feet in length, the loom being worked in a circular orbit to give the end of the blade a zigzag lifting pattern in the water. Although a single crewman can handle one efficiently, they are frequently worked by up to ten crewmen to each yuloh on middle-sized craft. The large broad-beamed junks will have twelve crewmen to each yuloh, giving relatively rapid forward progress. The models are provided with only a single pair of yulohs, but a large junk often carries up to a dozen yulohs for use in slack water when bound upstream or on a downstream journey. The yulohs and sails require storage on the lumber irons when the junk is working cargo in port.

A large *Shou-K'ou Ma-Yang-Tzu* on the Ichang-Chungking run normally carries a regular crew of about twelve men: the junk captain and his family, a purser, a hold-keeper, two quartermasters, a helmsman, a cook, four ordinary crewmen, and a head tracker. For the upbound journey anywhere from seventy to one hundred trackers, as the season and the state of the river requires, will be engaged to haul the junk over the rapids through the gorges. And dependent on the season, the state of the river, and the feeling of urgency of the junk captain, anywhere from ten to a hundred yuloh-men will be retained on the crew for the downstream journey.

PLATE 22. Shou-K'ou Ma-Yang-Tzu

I-CHANG MA-YANG-TZU

Variants of the *Shou-K'ou Ma-Yang-Tzu* formerly were built at Ichang, at the foot of the gorges, for
traffic into the lower gorges zone and to Shasi, downriver. These normally were smaller craft, seldom
over eighty feet long, equipped with a single main
mast, a shallow-water rudder, and a bow steering
boom. These junks were basically true to the *Shou-
K'ou Ma-Yang-Tzu* build, the most noticeable variant
being the narrow catwalk aft of the captain's cabin.

In this particular model the builder used solid
pieces of wood for the cabin roofs, representative of
an old junk on which the repeated tung oil coats
have produced a smooth and shiny black surface.
Tracking ropes seldom were stored on the cabin roofs
when the junk was working to Shasi.

The two long, pointed wood spars (in practice

twenty to twenty-five feet long) lashed to the second
and third crossbeams on the two *Shou-K'ou Ma-
Yang-Tzu* models and on this one, and also present
on a few other models in the collection, are carried
by many large junks as mooring spars. Large junks,
when in port, most often line up side by side, with
the bow against the shore and one or more hawsers
running ashore. But when a large junk must anchor
for the night alone, it lies near a bank with the bow
upstream. One mooring spar is then shoved into the
mud of the bank, with the inboard end lashed down
to a bow crossbeam, and the other spar is similarly
placed at one of the stern bumkins. Hawsers then
hold the junk inshore, as the mooring spars hold it
off the bank, riding on safe water. At least two head
ropes will run from the bow to stakes planted upstream, to prevent downstream drift.

PLATE 23. I-Chang Ma-Yang-Tzu

MA-YANG KUA-TZU-CH'UAN

Centuries ago passengers roughed it in traveling through the Yangtze Gorges in either direction. After the development of the *Shou-Kou Ma-Yang-Tzu* as a freight junk, its style was adapted for a passenger junk that provided relative safety and a degree of comfort. The *Ma-Yang Kua-Tzu-Ch'uan* normally carried some freight on all trips, having a capacity of twenty to thirty-five tons. The *Kua-Tzu-Ch'uan* were built from about sixty to one hundred feet in length, with a beam of fourteen to twenty feet but a depth of no more than five to six feet. A shallow-water rudder and a bow steering boom were normal features. These passenger junks normally carried a single sail, but this one sail was mounted on a very tall mast stepped farther forward than in the freight junks.

Junk models this large (forty-eight inches) were seldom constructed for the market trade, and this one was acquired a bit too early in the collecting phase, so it came with decoration in foreign paints. Since passenger junks normally did carry some decoration and latticed features, it is only the medium employed that makes this model untrue to type.

Steamship traffic through the Yangtze Gorges came much later than on the Yangtze below Ichang, but it did come, and that spelled the end of the passenger junks on the gorges section of the river. The journey from Ichang to Chungking by a *Kua-Tzu-Ch'uan* normally took from twenty-five to thirty-five days during winter low water, the passenger junks moving only during the day, hauling rapids slowly after all freight junks had passed up, and anchoring each night. During the summer high-water period the upbound trip, with flood freshets running, might take as many as fifty days. The downstream journey took anywhere from five to twelve days. When modern passenger steamers began the regular run from Ichang to Chungking in 1926, the upbound journey took three days, with anchoring at night, and the downbound journey required a day and a half to two days, dependent upon the speed of the current.

PLATE 24. Ma-Yang Kua-Tzu-Ch'uan

PA-TUNG HSIAO-HO-HUA-TZU

The standard concepts of Chinese watercraft become ineffective when the craft of very small and shallow streams are examined. The "Little River Small Boat" is often a conveyance peculiar to a single stream. Patung is the last town in Hupeh as one ascends the Yangtze River. About two miles above Patung a "little river" enters the Yangtze on the north bank. In the rainy season this may be a torrent of flood water, but much of the year it is a small stream of clear water alternately flowing through quiet reaches a few feet deep or noisily spilling over boulder-strewn gravel-bar rapids. In any state of water short of a flood freshet, a small boat may be used on the twenty-odd navigable miles of the lower "valley" section. I spent three days on this little stream at rather low water, two-and-a-half days upbound and about three hours downbound, in the small boat depicted in the model.

The *Pa-Tung Hsiao-Ho-Hua-Tzu* is a double-ended boat, pointed at either end, with sides about two feet high in the waist, almost three-and-a-half feet at either end, with a five-foot beam at the waist gunwale, and approximately twenty-three feet long. The model is a bit too smoothly presented, but the hull planking is lapped and worked relatively smooth inside and out, being constructed of heavy planks of cypress that run the full length of the hull on either side, with the hull flaring outward at all points. The ends of the hull are held together by driving double-ended heavy nails through the ends of both sets of planks, clinching both sets (not shown on the model). The bottom is flat, and the boat rides on about six inches of water when light. A large bamboo mat is bent into shape as a cabin roof, held in place behind four stanchions, any two of which also serve as ties for tracking lines when needed. Within the cabin section two bulkheads are set, topped by planking that provides a dry rest for perishable cargo. Neither ribs nor frames provide further support for the hull. Loose boards form a floor supported on cleats nailed to the hull. Four oars can be mounted, two at either end. A stick-in-the-mud anchor is boxed in at one end, but, since either end may point upstream on occasion, the end holding the anchor post may be termed either the prow or the stern.

On the upstream journey the four-man crew alternately rowed through the deeper reaches or were over the side pushing the boat over a rapid. On my trip no cargo was carried, and I was ashore at each rapid, so no tracking was necessary. On the downbound trip the whole crew rode, rowing through a reach and then guiding the course with the oars or fending off the gravel-bank margins with oars when bumping over a rapid.

This little craft moves up to a half-ton of general cargo upstream, although at some rapids at very low water some cargo must be portaged around the rapid. Downbound almost a ton of cargo can be carried in any reasonable water, contraband salt often occupying the high section within the cabin, salt that in the 1930's was being smuggled out of salt-well works from over the hills in eastern Szechwan into the Hupeh market zone. There is a bottom trail along the canyon, and also a high hill-trail, but most commodities move up or down the valley as boat cargo.

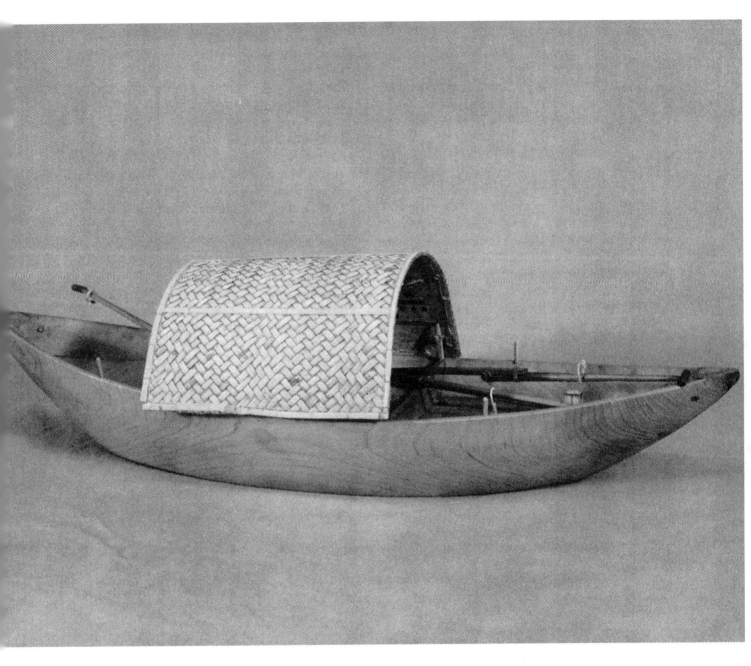

PLATE 25. Pa-Tung Hsiao-Ho-Hua-Tzu

HSIANG-CHI TOU-K'OU

From the village of Hsiang Chi and the nearby town of Tzekuei (sometimes listed on maps as Kweichow) in western Hupeh, within the Yangtze Gorges, there trades a stout little junk called the Hsiang-Chi Bean Pod, from its smooth and tapering lines and the planking that encloses the two cabins. It appears to have long been built locally, somewhat patterned after an older style of craft out of Hunan termed the *Shen-Po-Tzu* (not to be confused with the Wushan Fan Tail junk of the same name). The *Hsiang-Chi Tou-K'ou* is built about thirty-five to forty feet in length, with a beam not greater than six-and-a-half feet and never more than three feet in depth, some craft being even more shallow. A medium-sized crossbeam is built into the superstructure toward the bow, and a heavier crossbeam is similarly built in across the quarter, projecting as a bumkin on either side. A removable timber laid across the hull just aft of the mast carries the fulcrum points for two yulohs. In many cases there are holes for thole pins in the forward coaming and oars may be mounted for specific periods of propulsion.

The *Tou-K'ou* mounts a moderately sized single sail (large for the size of the craft) stepped just forward of midship, the mast having a slight stern rake. Just aft of the mast smooth planking is built up fairly high as cabin housing, this planking tapering both inward and upward toward the stern to fit around a high strong sternpost. The cabins are mat-covered. When new and clean, the *Tou-K'ou* is a most attractive little craft. It seldom handles more than a ton of cargo, but it is highly maneuverable on the thrashing waters within gorges and makes the trip both upstream to Wanhsien and downstream to Ichang.

PLATE 26. Hsiang-Chi Tou-K'ou

WU-SHAN SHEN-PO-TZU

One of the more interesting and gracefully built of all the river craft of the Yangtze River Basin is the Wushan Fan Tail, as it is known in English. The *Shen-Po-Tzu* is at least a thousand years old, and its style has remained traditionally similar during the millennium (it is not to be confused with an old Hunan junk style of the same name). The inward-curved high stern and the narrowing taper at both bow and stern somewhat resemble the lines of the *Ma-Ch'iao-Wei* (Sparrow Tail) originated by the Miao tribal navigators of the narrow and rapid-strewn upper Yuan River in western Hunan. The *Shen-Po-Tzu* originated on the Taning River, a north-bank tributary of the Yangtze in eastern Szechwan, and was designed to navigate the narrow reaches and shallow rocky rapids of the Taning. The sail is not used on the Taning, the craft riding the swift current downstream and being tracked upstream by a small crew assisted by three oarsmen. Owing to the shallowness of the water in and just above the rapids most of the year, the *Shen-Po-Tzu* does not mount a rudder when working the Taning but is steered by a stern sweep fastened on the port gunwale at the upward curve of the stern. The fan tail serves to prevent shipping water over the stern in riding a rapid downstream and provides a good pushing point in moving the junk over a shallow on the upstream trip, since crewmen then often enter the water to help maneuver the junk past the obstacle.

The *Shen-Po-Tzu* normally travel in groups of six to a dozen junks for purposes of mutual assistance and protection on the Taning, the eastern Szechwan

mountain country having a long tradition of local banditry. Although specially built for use on the Taning River, fleets of *Shen-Po-Tzu* trade the ports of the Yangtze between Ichang and Wanhsien. They are to be seen on the Yangtze particularly during mid-summer, when high water and peculiar current patterns just above each rapid make the Taning too dangerous for navigation. When on the big river the junks mount a fairly large Ichang-type sail and also a fairly large full-balance rudder. All *Shen-Po-Tzu* carry full sets of movable mat shelters amidship on the cabin roof, and one of the distinctive rainy-day sights of the river ports between Ichang and Wanhsien is a little fleet of Fan Tails anchored side by side, nosing in against the shore, covered from stem to stern with the mats in sheltering position. Another distinctive feature is the stick-in-the-mud anchor post, dropped through a simple hole in the hull just above the water line in the stern. This allows a junk to ride up or down the post with any change in water level while maintaining position.

Always built between thirty-five and fifty-five feet in length, with a five-and-a-half to six-foot beam, and three to four feet in depth, the junks are rather light, with a hull of relatively thin planking but reinforced by eleven to fifteen bulkheads which provide support. The mast is stepped fairly far forward and is sometimes kept in place when the junk is bound upstream on the Taning, to serve in tracking. When working the Taning River the largest junks carry downstream cargoes of almost two tons on a fifteen- to eighteen-inch draft, but upward bound cargoes run under a ton per junk on an eight- to ten-inch draft. Light, the *Shen-Po-Tzu* rides on five to seven inches of water.

PLATE 27. Wu-Shan Shen-Po-Tzu

WAI-P'I-KU

The Wu, or Kungt'an, River, is a tributary of the Yangtze, flowing out of Kweichow, with its mouth at Fouling, on the south bank, sixty-five miles below Chungking. There are five separately navigable sections of the Wu, each with its own locally built fleet of junks, since boats cannot navigate the rapids that create the five units. On the uppermost section boats are "normal," but on all four lower sections crooked-stern junks are used. Salt is the chief commodity freighted upstream, and but little moves downstream. Below the town of Kungt'an, at the head of the final section, the stream drops 1,200 feet in 200 miles, and there are seventy-one rapids. There are two styles of crooked-stern junk, a large and a small one.

The large crooked-stern junk is built from seventy to ninety feet in length, with a beam of sixteen to nineteen feet and a depth of five to six feet. The bottom and hull are built of either cedrela or maple, with other elements built of fir. It probably is the most crudely built large junk of any produced in the Yangtze Basin; despite that, the craft is sturdy and achieves a practical solution to the problems of the difficult waters of the Wu. The bow has a long high lift well out of water, and the line of the port gunwale is a continuous curve from bow to stern, but the starboard gunwale shows less curve, since it reaches a lower position on the stern. The main cabin is long and high, the sides built halfway up of wood and then roofed in matting. Standing over the cabin is a wobbly flying bridge that often is twenty feet or more above the water.

The crooked-stern junk mounts no sail or rudder but employs one long bow sweep and two stern sweeps; the overall length from tip to tip of the sweeps ranges between 155 and 190 feet on different sized junks. Many features are ill-fitting, crooked, and rickety about the Wai-P'i-Ku, and the cracks between planks are never caulked above the waterline, but the outstanding feature, of course, is the very crooked shape of the stern and the very curious mounting of the two stern sweeps. The port corner of the taffrail is several feet above the starboard corner and also further aft, but that port corner stands along the longitudinal centerline of the junk, as necessary for steering efficiency. The big stern sweep is operated from the flying bridge and the second stern sweep from the main afterdeck, so that each operates on a different radius in a separate plane, without conflict.

The model presents the general form of the large Wai-P'i-ku, but it must be considered only generally illustrative of the style, since some items are in error. The model is too smoothly put together, the bow is too thick and does not lift enough, the stern is rounded rather than making the sharp angular break at the bend in the planking from the bottom to the stern, there should not be a stick-in-the-mud anchor post, and the tracking mast is placed too far into the waist and is twice too tall. I had not seen a Wai-P'i-Ku when the model was purchased; I later traveled on four of them downstream bound but never had an opportunity to have another model built. A possible explanation for the construction of the stern is given in the introduction (see p. 31).

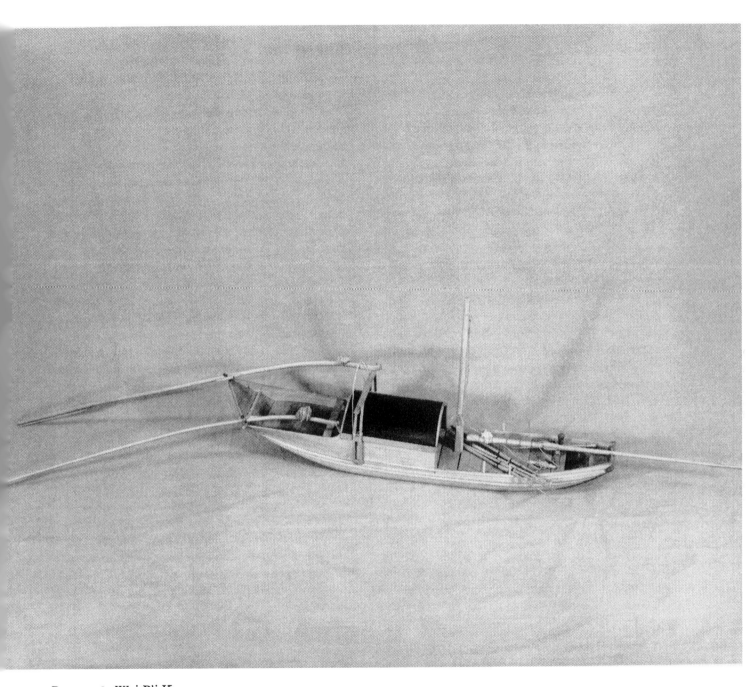

PLATE 28. Wai-P'i-Ku

LAO-HUA-CH'IU

The largest junk working any of the rivers of
Szechwan is the *Lao-Hua-Ch'iu*, built particularly for
navigating the Suining River of northern Szechwan,
a west-bank tributary of the Kialing River. The
Suining drains the central northern portion of
Szechwan, and the Kialing joins the Yangtze River
at Chungking. The craft do come down the Kialing
to Chungking occasionally, but chiefly they transship
their cargo at Hochow at the mouth of the Suining.
The *Lao-Hua-Ch'iu* is a general cargo carrier, and
the larger craft handle about eighty tons on about
three feet of water downstream but rarely carry more
than fifty tons on the upstream journey.

Usually built between 100 and 130 feet in length,
with a beam of 14 to 17 feet, these craft are rather
shallow, seldom being 5 feet in depth. The hull is
turret-built on an angular pattern in which the widest
point of beam is normally just below waterline when
a junk is well loaded, so that the upper sides of the
hull slant inward from the waterline to the flush
foredeck, which is protected by coaming. The top
planks of the hull are lapped from above and the bottom hull planks from below, reaching the angular
wide point of the beam in a final filler-plank. The
hull is more lightly built than on many junks and is
of cypress, whereas the bottom is planked of oak.
The bow tapers slightly but has only a slight lift,
whereas the stern lifts smoothly to a level often ten
feet above the water. Both cabins are built of wood
and are mat-covered (the solid black cover on the
model represents old matting). The *Lao-Hua-Ch'iu*

has smooth clean lines and an attractive appearance.

All junks in this style employ a bow stick-in-
the-mud anchor. On either side of the anchor box
are two short, strong bollards that serve as the initial
tie-points for tracking lines, which then run back
along the deck to be made fast on the single bumkin
on either side of the hull just aft of the main cabin.
Tracking lines must sometimes be used to warp a
junk around a sharp curve on an upbound voyage
when a strong freshet is running. Eight oars are the
normal complement for propulsion because, although
the sail may be of some value, winds are not very
reliable in the Szechwan Basin. Tracking a well-
loaded junk on an upbound journey is necessary on
certain reaches of the Suining. These craft carry
waterproof mats to cover the whole foredeck and the
between-cabins open space when it rains.

The *Lao-Hua-Ch'iu* is the only true Szechwan
junk in the collection mounting a sail, but it illustrates the cotton square sail now used on all craft
whose home port is above Wanhsien. This sail has no
battens, parrels, or multiple sheets such as are used
on the lug sails down river. The sail is laced to a top
yard and to a bottom yard that extends beyond the
sail on the port side. Near the end of this yard a
small peg is angled into the yard (missing on the
model). As one crewman cuts loose the diagonally
secured backstay and then lets the top yard down
about three feet, another crewman uses the peg to
roll the sail fully onto the bottom yard; the top yard
is then slightly off vertical, but the bottom yard and
sail stand vertically beside the mast, out of the way.

PLATE 29. Lao-Hua-Ch'iu

Selective Bibliographic Notes

T HERE are some technical studies of coastal sea-going Chinese junks and a few popular books and articles on the sea-going craft, but there are very few pieces of writing that deal with the freshwater craft. The following list is not exhaustive, but it is most of what there is.

Audemard, L. *Les Jonques Chinoises.* Rotterdam: Publicaties van het Museum Voor Land- en Volkenkunde en het Maritiem Museum "Prins Hendrik," 1957–1965. Comander Audemard spent most of the years 1902–1910 on duty on the Yangtze River, but his manuscript turned up only in 1948. The work consists of six paperback monographs totaling 512 pages on the history, ornamentation, cataloguing, and construction of Chinese junks, chiefly those of the Yangtze Basin, including hundreds of pen drawings and sketches of types from the Yangtze Delta to western Szechwan, done at a time prior to the disappearance of many of the types.

Donnelly, Ivan A. *Chinese Junks and Other Native Craft.* Shanghai: Kelly & Walsh, 1924, 1930. 142 pages. Brief text and pictures or drawings of each of thirty-one junk types, but only two are of Yangtze River types.

Le Palud, A. M. *The Yangtze Gorges in Pictures and Prose.* Shanghai: Kelly & Walsh, undated (about 1934). Eighteen pages of text narrate a steamer trip through the Yangtze Gorges, and there are fifty-seven full-page photographs of the gorges and some junks seen within the gorges.

Little, Archibald John. *Through the Yangtze Gorges, or Trade and Travel in Western China.* London: Sampson Low, Marston, Searle, and Rivington, 1888. 368 pages. Essentially the journal of a trip from Shanghai to Chungking and return in an era when powered craft had made few inroads on the junk trade and before any powered vessels navigated the gorges. Extensive notes on junk types on the Upper River.

Moore, W. Robert. "Along the Yangtze, Main Street of China." *National Geographic* 93 (1948), 325–356. Interesting photographs of many aspects of life along the river, including watercraft.

Spencer, J. E. "Down the Wukiang by Crooked Stern Junk." *The China Journal* 32 (1940), 55–60. A narrative of a trip down the river on a *Wai-P'i-Ku*, with ten photographs.

———. "The Junks of the Yangtze." *Asia* 38 (1938), 466–470. A popular article illustrating some of the models in the collection, plus other photographs.

Worcester, G. R. G. *The Floating Population of China.* Hong Kong: Vetch and Lee, 1970. 90 pages. The first fifty pages cover chiefly coastal sea-going junk types, but there are three Yangtze River craft. The second portion of the book consists of pen sketches of particular spots on the Yangtze River done by Doris Worcester.

———. *The Junks and Sampans of the Yangtze.* Annapolis, Md.: Naval Institute Press, 1971. 626 pages. This is a revised and reprinted version of the original four volumes published by the Chinese Maritime Customs, Shanghai, 1940–1948, and is the definitive work on the watercraft of the Yangtze Basin. It contains textual discussion, plans and specifications, maps, drawings, photographs, and comments on a wide range of "things Chinese."

———. *Sail and Sweep in China.* London: Her Majesty's Stationery Office, 1966. 146 pages. Essentially summarized material from Worcester's original four volumes, this has notes on and pictures of most of the twenty-seven items in the collection of Chinese watercraft in the British Science Museum, but they are chiefly of sea-going craft.

Index

anchor, 40; cable, 54, 60; capstan, 52, 68; stick-in-the-mud, 44, 88, 92, 94, 96
anchoring, 62, 72, 84
animism, 74
awning, 62, 66, 72

banditry, 92
beam, width of. *See individual junk styles*
boat-building. *See* construction of junks
boat-hooking, 68, 72
boat races, 74
bollards, 54, 60, 66, 68, 70, 96
bow, 44, 60, 78, 94; coaming, 52, 62; high, 40, 44, 46; pointed, 88; square, 68; steering boom, 84, 86; sweep, 94; tapering, 48, 52, 72, 96; twisted, 31–33
British Science Museum, 37
bulkheads, 60, 72, 88, 92; construction of, 36; in Dragon Boat design, 74; extra, 42; fewer than normal, 50, 62, 64; pumping out, 70
bumkins, 32, 48, 80, 90, 96

cabin, 42, 50, 86; decoration of, 46; enclosed by planking, 90; mat roofing of, 22, 44–54 *passim*, 60, 82, 88, 90, 94, 96; ladders atop, 80, 86; passenger, 46; removed, 62; removable roof panels of, 40, 54, 56; of river and coastal junks compared, 22; solid wood, 40, 52, 78; stern, 46, 50-56 *passim,* 60, 64, 66, 80; tracking lines atop, 80, 84; wood, 44, 52, 54, 60, 94, 96; wood roofs of, 52, 84; wood sides of, 48, 56. *See also* house

canals, 17, 64
cannon, 66
cargo: capacity of river and coastal junks, 20; on passenger junks, 86; transferred by lighter, 70
—commodities: general cargo, 40, 42, 50–60, 76, 90; specific, 17, 40, 42, 62, 64, 68. *See also* salt as cargo
—maximum capacity in tons: five and under, 44, 62, 64, 76, 88, 90, 92; nine to fourteen, 54; twenty, 64; thirty, 48, 50, 52; thirty-five, 42, 86; forty, 60; sixty, 70; sixty-five, 40; eighty, 96; one hundred or more, 70, 80
cargo lighter, 70
carpenters, 33–35
cathead, 54, 60
catwalk, 60, 84
caulking, 30, 36, 94
channels, 21, 29, 44, 46, 64; flood, 17, 24, 26. *See also* Pien Ho
China Sea, 21
Chinese Imperial Post Office, 78
Chinkiang, 20–21
Ch'iu-Tzu (class of junk), 52, 54
Ch'u state of, 74
Chungking, 24, 94; boat-building in, 29–30; junk styles in waters of, 44, 60, 76, 80, 82, 86, 96; rapids near, 28, 29; in Upper River zone, 20, 78
Ch'u Yuan, 74
coal, 17, 42
coaming, 60, 62, 64, 66, 90; foredeck, 40, 42, 50, 72, 96; stern, 48
coffer-dam, 70
commodities. *See* cargo
Communist China, 20
construction of junks: craftsmanship in, 23–24, 30–31, 94; described, 36;

of estuarine zone craft, 21–22; non-Chinese origins of, 24; of river and coastal junks compared, 20, 21–22; traditions in, 17, 33; wood used in, 33–36. *See also specific parts of boats;* styles of junks
creeks, 56, 58, 62, 88. *See also* streams
crews, 44, 50, 76, 82; navigating streams, 88; of police junk, 66; of retail trader, 62; of river and coastal junks compared, 20; of sampan, 72
crooked-stern junk, 31–33, 36, 94
crossbeams, 46, 60, 68, 78, 84, 90; heavy, 48; removable, 50, 52, 54, 64
Cunninghamia (fir), 34
customs, 66, 78

decoration of junks, 21–22, 82; Dragon Boats, 74; passenger junks, 46, 86; river and coastal junks compared, 20
dike system, 24, 26
Dragon Boat Festival, 74
Dragon King, 74

elevation, changes in, 17, 26, 94
Empire, the, 66
estuarine transition zone, 20–21, 22, 23

Fan-Kuan-Ch'uan (class of junk), 68
Fan Tail (class of junk), 90, 92
Fast Crabs (class of junk), 66
Fei-Hsieh (class of junk), 66
ferrying, 72, 76
fittings, construction of, 36
flying bridge, 32, 33, 94
folk religion, 74

Fouling, 94
freight. *See* cargo

galley, 66
gangway, poling. *See* poling gangway
garbage chute, 80
grain tribute junks, 23
gods, river, 74
government: imperial, 66, 78; modern, 20, 74
Grand Canal, 22, 23
Gulf of Pohai, 20
gunwale, 60, 88, 92, 94

Hankow (Wuhan), 40, 52, 58; cargo lighter of, 70; coal freighted to, 42; in Lower River zone, 20, 23; messenger junks to, 46
—in trade routes: Hankow-Chungking, 76; Hankow-Ichang, 20, 26, 60, 64; Hankow-Shanghai, 23; Hunan ports–Hankow, 24; Laohok'ou-Hankow, 25, 52
Han River, 26, 58, 64; described, 24–25; junk styles of, 25, 52, 54
Hart, Robert, 79
hawsers, 66, 84
Hochow, 96
holds, 42, 46, 50, 72, 76, 78
Honan, 24
house, 22, 30, 36, 50, 68
houseboats, 68
Hsiang Chi, 90
Hsiang-Chi Bean Pod, 90
Hsiangyang, 25, 54
H'uai, Prince, 74
Hua-Tzu (class of junk), 56, 58, 62, 72, 88
hull: construction of, 36; converted to tea house, 68; decoration of, 74; slants inward, 48, 80, 96; thickened, 44; thin, 92, 96; turret-built, 48, 80, 96. *See also* bow; crossbeams; planking; stern; timber; wales
Hunan Province, 30, 74; salt distribution in, 48
—junk styles of: compared to Szechwan style, 31; described, 23–24; on Han River, 25; *Ma-Yang-Tzu*, 56, 80; models of, 37; as origin of other styles, 25, 26, 29, 56, 80; *Pa-Kan*, 46; *Pien-Tzu*, 54, 56, 64; police junk, 66; salt junk, 48
Hupeh Province, 24, 30, 34, 74, 80; junk styles of, 23, 54, 66, 88, 90,

92; models of junks of, 37; Yangtze Gorges tracking in, 26–27

Ichang, 17, 34, 36; as base port for river police, 66; boat race, 74; cargo lighters, 70; floating restaurants and tea houses, 68; Ichang-Chungking message carrier, 76; *Ma-Yang-Tzu* of, 84; *Pien-Tzu* built at, 64; in Postal Boat range, 78; sampan, 62, 70, 72, 78; steamship traffic, 86; type of sail, 66, 78, 92; in Yangtze River zones, 20, 24, 26, 29
—in trade routes: Ichang-Chungking, 29, 82, 86; Ichang-Hankow, 60, 64; Ichang-Shasi, 76, 82; Ichang-Wanhsien, 90, 92
Ichang (Lampshine) Gorge, 27, 66
inns, floating, 68

junks: broad-beamed, 54, 56, 64, 66, 68, 82; decreasing numbers of, 20; double-ended, 88; flat-bottomed, 20, 88; highly maneuverable, 72, 76, 90; river and coastal compared, 20–22; shallow-water, 24, 66, 72, 88, 90; traveling in groups, 92. *See also* construction of junks; navigation conditions; styles of junks; trade routes; traffic patterns
—propulsion other than sail: boathooking, 68, 72; pushing by crew, 88, 92. *See also* oars; poling; tracking; yulohs
—uses of: cargo lighter, 70; ferrying, 72, 76; houseboats, inns, restaurants, tea houses, 68; message carrier, 46; military and police junks, 66; passenger carrier, 46, 86; postal boat, 29, 78; racing, 74. *See also* cargo
Junks and Sampans of the Yangtze, The, 37

Kan River, 40
Kialing River, 22, 29, 96
Kiangsi Province, 23, 40
Kiangsu, 22
Kiukiang, 23
Kungt'an River, 31, 94
Kwanghwa, 24, 25, 52
Kweichow, 90, 94

lakes: watercraft of, 22, 23-24; small, shallow, 17, 26, 56, 58, 62; in

Yangtze River system, 23–24. *See also* Poyang Lake; Tungting Lake
Lampshine Gorge, 66
land transportation, 17, 26, 58, 62
Laohok'ou, 24, 25, 52
leeboards, 21
lighter, cargo, 35, 70
little rivers: junk styles of, 88
Lower River (Yangtze), 20–26
Luchou, 80
lumber irons, 25, 40, 52, 60, 82
Lung-Ch'uan (class of junk), 74
Lung Wang, 74
Lu River, 29

Ma-Ch'iao-Wei (Sparrow Tail), 92
mail, 78
masts: of river and coastal junks compared, 22; two, 40, 44, 54, 60, 64, 80; three, 80
—single, 44, 48, 56, 58, 62, 66, 84; far forward, 42, 50; short, 42; slight stern rake of, 90; used in tracking, 92; very tall, 86
mat, bamboo: cabin, 42; cabin roof, 44–52 *passim*, 60, 82, 88, 90, 94, 96; covers, 48, 58, 92, 96
Mayang, 80
Ma-Yang-Tzu (class of junk), 68; features of, in other styles, 46, 48, 56, 60, 64, 68, 78; Upper River styles of, 29, 80–86
messenger junk, 46
Miao tribal navigators, 92
Middle River (Yangtze), 17, 20, 26, 29, 56
military junk, 66
Min River, 29
models of junks: accuracy of, 37, 42, 66, 74, 88, 94; collections of, 37; decoration of, 82, 86
mooring, 84

Nanking, 23, 40
navigation conditions: creeks, 56, 58, 62, 72, 88; crowded waterways, 52; shallows, 40, 52, 78, 92; small, shallow lakes, 17, 26, 56, 58, 62; streams, 17, 20, 29, 30, 40, 72, 88. *See also* canals; channels; elevation, changes in; lakes; rapids; water level, seasonal variation in
Ningpo, 22
North China, 20

oars, 58, 68, 78, 96; sampan, 72; retail trader, 62; police junk, 66. *See also* yulohs
oarsmen, 24

paddlers, 74
Pai-Mu-Ch'uan, 80
Pa-Kan (class of junk), 46
passenger junks, 46, 86
passenger steamers, 68, 72
Patung, 88
Pa-Wan-Ch'uan (class of junk), 27
Pien Ho, 26, 54, 58, 62, 64
Pien-Tzu (class of junk), 54, 64; in other styles, 56
pilots: navigate rapids, 29
Pingshan, 17
planking: 40, 70, 92; as coaming, 48, 90; construction of, 36; enclosing cabin, 90; smooth, 44, 88; woods used for, 36, 42, 60, 74, 88, 96
police junks, 66
poling, 52, 56, 64, 68
poling gangway, 50, 54, 56, 60; as feature of inland craft, 22; unusual, 46, 64, 66
Postal Administration, 78
Postal Boat, 29, 78
Poyang Lake, 20, 23, 24, 40

quanting poles, 52

races, 74
rapids: 24, 76, 80, 82; Kan River, 40; on streams, 30, 88; Taning River, 92; Wu River, 31, 32, 94. *See also* tracking; Yangtze Gorges
restaurant, floating, 68
ribs, 36, 88
roof: over tiller room, 40. *See also* cabin
rubbing strakes, 52, 54, 62
rudder, 31, 70, 72, 92; construction of, 35, 36; of river and coastal junks compared, 20, 21, 22; shallow-water, 44, 62, 66, 78, 84, 86

Sail and Sweep in China, 37
sails, 36, 50, 52, 76, 90; Ichang-style, 66, 78, 92; none, 31, 94; of passenger junks, 46, 86; of river and coastal junks compared, 20, 22; square, Szechwan-style, 30, 96;

storage of, 40, 58, 78, 82; striped, 66; three. 80. *See also* masts
salt as cargo, 22–23; contraband, 88; craft designed for, 17, 31, 48, 50; on Wu River, 31, 32
Salt Revenue Administration, 48
sampan, 37; defined, 76; Ichang, 62, 70, 72, 78; tender, 40
Shanghai, 23, 24, 70
Shasi, 24, 50, 54; inland waterways near, 58, 64, 72; junks based at, 26, 56, 58, 62; in junk traffic patterns, 56, 66, 72, 76, 80, 84
Shen-Po-Tzu (class of junk), 90, 92
Shou-K'ou Ma-Yang-Tzu (class of junk), 28, 29, 37, 80, 82; rudder of, 35; variant of, 82
Shui-Pao-Chia, 66
South China, 20
Sparrow Tail, 92
spars, 84
steam-powered watercraft: junks serving, in port, 68, 70, 72; towing of junks by, 54
—effect of, on junks, 20, 22–23; on specific junk types, 40, 46, 50, 78, 80, 86
steering boom, 46, 78, 84, 86
steering sweep, 32, 76, 92, 94
stern, 44, 68, 74; awning of, 62, 72; cabin on, 46, 50–56 *passim,* 60, 64, 66, 80; crooked, 31–33, 36, 94; high, 42, 92, 96; mat covers for, 48, 58, 96; pointed, 88; post of, 42, 52, 90; steering boom of, 46, 78; steering sweep of, 76, 92, 94; tapering, 42, 48, 52, 72, 78, 90, 92; transom, 62, 70, 72, 78
streams, 17, 20, 29, 30, 88. *See also* creeks
styles of junks: factors determining, 17, 29, 30–31, 42, 48; models of, 37; modified, 60; number of, in Yangtze Basin, 19–20; twisted bow and crooked stern, 31–33. *See also* Hunan Province; Hupeh Province; Szechwan Province
—and families: in estuarine transition zone, 22–23; in lower Han River, 25; in Middle Yangtze, 26; in Upper Yangtze, 28–29; in Wuhu-Hankow Yangtze River section, 23
—hybrid, 23, 25, 26, 29; specific junks, 48, 54, 56, 64, 78
Suining River, 96

Szechwan Province, 22, 26, 34, 80, 88; junk styles of, 29, 31, 92, 96; mail route to, 78

taffrail, 94
Taiping Rebellion, 66
Taning River, 92
Tao-Pa-Tzu (class of junk), 27
taxes, 17, 42, 48
tea houses, floating, 68
tide, 21
timber: as cargo, 17; in junk construction, 33–36
—specific kinds: cedrela, 36, 94; cypress, 34, 36, 42, 60, 80, 82, 96; fir, 34, 36, 42, 50, 52, 54, 60, 62, 74; juniper, 34; laurel, 36, 48, 72; maple, 36, 94; oak, 33–34, 96
Tou-K'ou, 90
towing, 29, 54, 72
tracking, 78, 80, 82, 84; of crooked-stern junk, 31–32, 94; along Yangtze River Gorges, 26–29; on other rivers, 31–32, 92, 94, 96; on streams, 30, 88
trade routes: of Han River junks, 25; in hinterlands between Yangtze and Han rivers, 26; of Hunan-style junks, 24; of Poyang Lake junks, 23; of Tungting Lake–Hunan region, 23–24; of Szechwan-style junks, 29–31
—Yangtze River sections: estuarine transition zone, 21, 22–23; Middle Yangtze, 26; Yangtze Gorges, 28–29; Ichang-Chungking, 26; Hankow-Ichang, 26; Wuhu-Hankow, 23
—of specific junks: Hankow-Inchang, 60, 64; Han River, 52, 54; Ichang-Chungking, 60, 78, 80, 82, 86; Ichang-Shasi, 84; Ichang-Szechwan, 78; Laohok'ou-Hankow, 52; lower Hunan rivers, 64; Kialing River, 96; lower Yangtze Gorges, 56; Middle Yangtze, 50, 56; northern Hunan, 48; Patung area streams, 88; Pien Ho, 54, 58, 62, 64; Poyang Lake, Nanking-Hankow, 40; Shasi area, 54–64 *passim,* 72; Shasi-Luchou, 80; Suining River, 96; Taning River, 92; Tungting Lake, 44, 56, 64; Tungting Lake, Hankow, Yuan River, 46; Tzu River, Tungting Lake, Hankow, 42;

Wanhsien-Chungking, 44; Wanh-sien-Ichang, 90, 92; Wu River, 94; Yochow-Shasi, 50

traders: European, 78; retail, 62

traffic patterns: converge at Shasi, 56; of estuarine transition zone, 22–23; and interport traffic, 68, 70, 72, 74, 76; overlapping, in Middle River, 26; of passenger boats, 46, 86; of postal boats, 78; of river police, 66

tung oil, 21, 36, 72, 82, 84

Tungting Lake, 48, 50, 58, 74; described, 24; junk styles navigating, 23–24, 42, 44, 46, 56, 64; as part of Middle River, 20, 26

Tzekuei (Kweichow), 90, 94

Tzeliutsing, 31

Tzu River, 42

Upper River (Yangtze), 20, 26–31, 78, 80–86

Wai-P'i-Ku (class of junk), 30; navigation of, 31–33, 94

wales, 64, 68, 78; along flanks of hull, 56; as rubbing strakes, 54, 62; symbolic, 58; three full-length, 70, 80; heavy, length of hull, 42, 50, 60, 76

Wanhsien, 22, 26, 28, 34, 44, 96; as junk-building center, 29–30, 86; in Postal Boat route, 78; Wanhsien-Ichang trade route, 90, 92

washboards, 54, 56, 60

water level, seasonal variation in; along Yangtze, 17, 26, 28, 70, 72, 86; of lakes, 17, 23, 24, 44, 58; of other rivers, 17, 31, 52, 54, 88, 92

weapons on junks, 66

wood. *See* timber

Worcester, G. R. G., 20, 31, 37

World War II, 29

Wuhan. *See* Hankow

Wuhu, 20–21, 22, 23

Wu-Pan (class of junk), 30; defined, 76: in other styles, 78

Wu (Kungt'an) River, 31, 94

Wushan, 31

Wushan Fan Tail, 90, 92

Ya-Shao (class of junk), 34

Yangtze Basin, 17, 19–20, 33–34

Yangtze Delta, 17, 20

Yangtze Gorges, 17, 24; navigation of, 26–29; trade junks navigating, 29, 44, 56, 80–84, 90; other junks navigating, 29, 66, 78, 86

Yangtze River: estuarine transition zone of, 20–23; head of navigation of, 17; river system of, 17; sections of, 17, 20; sedimentation of, 24–25; tributaries of, 17, 29, 88, 92, 94, 96 (*see also specific rivers*). See also Lower River; Middle River; Upper River

Yangtze Valley, 66

Yochow, 48, 50

Yuan River, 29, 46, 48, 80, 92

yulohs, 35, 68, 76; described, 40, 82. *See also* oars

—pivot for: removable crossbeams as, 50, 52, 54, 64; stationary crossbeams as, 46, 48; swing-out beams as, 40

CPSIA information can be obtained
at www.ICGtesting.com
Printed in the USA
BVHW011013080620
581025BV00009B/332